CHEAP SHELTER

CHEAP SHELTER

David Carter

 Sterling Publishing Co., Inc.
Distributed in the U.K. by Blandford Press

Edited and designed by Barbara Busch.

Library of Congress Cataloging in Publication Data

Carter, David.
    Cheap shelter.

    Includes index.
    1. House construction.   2. Dwellings.   I. Title.
TH4812.C37 1984   690'.81   84-2759
ISBN 0-8069-7896-1 (pbk.)

Copyright © 1984 by David Carter
Published by Sterling Publishing Co., Inc.
Two Park Avenue, New York, N.Y. 10016
Distributed in Australia by Oak Tree Press Co., Ltd.
P.O. Box K514 Haymarket, Sydney 2000, N.S.W.
Distributed in the United Kingdom by Blandford Press
Link House, West Street, Poole, Dorset BH15 1LL, England
Distributed in Canada by Oak Tree Press Ltd.
% Canadian Manda Group, P.O. Box 920, Station U
Toronto, Ontario, Canada M8Z 5P9
Manufactured in the United States of America
All rights reserved

Contents

Foreword

With the exception of the West, shelter is a very personal experience throughout most of the world. Technology and specialization have depersonalized our shelter considerations. Few of us design or plan our own shelter. Leaving shelter to the "specialists" has also removed the criteria that in many cases make a shelter economic, energy-efficient, and even attractive. It is to be hoped that this book will once again make planning your personal abode one of the most important and enjoyable experiences of your life.

Acknowledgments

It is difficult at best to give credit for any creative endeavor since the knowledge and learned skills necessary are an accumulation of a lifetime of contributions by many people. My own attitudes were shaped in large part by my parents during my childhood.

My friends Chuck Sales, Jim Brown, Gary Everett, Warren Gilbert and Steve Bengston are always a source of encouragement and help me to not take myself too seriously. My loving companion, Debra, and my children, Heidi, Leslie and Julie, give me the best environment possible for creating, and my father, who is approaching ninety years, leaves his sunshine on my sometimes rather dusty path.

Special credit goes to my friend Chuck Sales, not only for his contribution of several illustrations that lend additional personality to these pages, but also for being a good listener. Having him listen to my rantings over the year this book has taken to compile provided a release for my emotions that gave me the clearer vision to continue.

To everyone else who has smiled at me on my journey, thanks for that wonderful gift.

CHEAP SHELTER

1

An Historical Perspective

The earliest men painted designs and otherwise tried to personalize their dwellings. Shelter adaptation and design was one of man's first creative acts and has always represented man's current culture as well as the innovations passed along by his ancestors, which increased both the livability and the efficiency of the structure. Until the industrial revolution, man was forced to cooperate with nature in order to survive and enjoy reasonable comfort. Everything seems to have come full circle, and once again man has the choice of cooperating with nature or paying a terrible price for his arrogance.

As man enlarged his occupation of the earth, he encountered formidable housing barriers. Climate extremes and material shortages forced innovation. Man's adaptability is the reason he survived. His earliest experiments with natural shelters such as caves remained a vestigial memory as areas without these shelters were inhabited. Tunisia and other arid lands were manually tunnelled since little other material for shelter was available. Man was first a food gatherer and usually stayed near ready sources of food, fuel and shelter. Rivers provided these amenities along with drinking water. These same rivers later became water highways for further exploration and settlement. Man's mobility meant the need for less permanent shelter, so as he became a hunter, he observed the home-building techniques of the birds and the animals he stalked.

Clusters of small trees and shrubs bent and tied together at the center of a small clearing formed an umbrella to shed water and give shade during the heat of the day. Observing the birds' use of mud, grass and twigs in building their nests led to man's use of these same materials, such as thatching over the bent-limb structure. Later, the use of mud bricks laid in a circle, narrowing to a smoke opening at the top to resemble a beehive or inverted mud nest came into prominence. Packed earth walls, stone masonry, cordwood, log, hide- and cloth-covered frames and other innovations multiplied along with population. Adaptations for the use of all of these materials found on site or fabricated from materials grown or sewn sprang up and are still in use throughout the world in one form or another.

13

Man also learned to design and adapt indigenous materials to best cope with the prevailing climate. Hot arid or humid climates dictated the use of shaded ventilated space while cold climates called for shelter that effectively shut the wind out and gave a certain amount of density to slow cold penetration and heat loss. Sod served the American Indian on the plains as well as the early pioneers as the ideal self-insulating building material.

After the consideration of climate, the material available dictated building designs. In most cases, the climate helps provide the materials—or the lack of them. Hot, arid regions have limited trees and little grass so dirt and rock prevail as the best medium. Tropical climes have an abundance of grasses, trees, and vegetation to construct high, airy and shaded space. The nomads who depend on their sheep and goats developed skin and cloth coverings for light frames and thus could easily follow their flocks to new pastures.

Man's social customs, religion and physical habits also came into play, and various cultures tended to develop distinctive shelter designs. The industrial revolution, and the development of the internal combustion engine, gave Western society great mobility and led to the export of material out of native areas into areas that lacked that particular material. This led to the creation of the mass production of frame houses throughout the United States and the decimation of its timber lands. In spite of heavy replanting programs, the ever-increasing demand outstrips the forests' abilities to recover.

Only an ongoing program to educate our population about systems, which better utilize indigenous materials, will help eliminate these problems. Our financial wealth has been misappropriated in large measure through the creation of home designs that for the most part require large amounts of dimensional lumber, concrete and masonry. These materials also require large amounts of capital to produce and transport. Modernized systems for incorporating the soil itself into wall-forming units would eliminate a large portion of these capital-intensive materials and reduce the skilled labor requirements, which add to the cost of construction. Rammed-earth or pisé is very durable, quite attractive and can be used in just about any design available. This material is both energy efficient and fireproof.

The West needs to concentrate its resources on developing building systems that use on-site materials, cooperate with the environment (solar orientation, wind energy, and the like) and can employ large numbers of unskilled laborers. This would reduce the cost of shelter, ease unemployment and conserve our unrenewable energy resources. In order to accomplish these goals, however, a major overhaul of the building codes is now necessary. The intent of these regulations is admirable, but the enforcement of them tends to benefit the building trades and material suppliers and inhibit innovation. Protecting the buying public is good but it could be accomplished without the protectionism of the stagnating building trades and suppliers who refuse to face the reality of economics. A performance-based code structure would protect the public and encourage innovation. Performance-based simply states an end result that is desired but does not limit the means of accomplishing it. For instance, instead of telling how high, wide and tall a window must be for egress from a bedroom, it could simply state that unimpeded egress directly to the outside of the structure must be provided for any inhabited area such as bedrooms. In lieu of this a corridor affording protection from fire and smoke must be provided to reach the outside of the structure. Any means then used to accomplish egress would have to prove its effectiveness. Inspection would have to be upgraded through better training and understanding of developing systems. A continuing education program of alternative energy systems and devices, along with research in developing the technology for using indigenous and alternative building materials is now a necessity. The end result of this will be tremendous innovation, reduced energy usage, personalized shelter, increased employment and lower costs.

As a base for all codes to rest upon, the following twelve criteria for energy-efficient building should be met.

1. Proper solar orientation.
2. Glazing oriented for maximum heat gain in winter and proper shading for summer (reduced glazing on west and north).
3. Soil pipe and thermal chimney cooling and dehumidification where applicable.
4. Heavy insulation including outside of basement walls and under footings/basement floors, where climate dictates.
5. Isolated mass within the structure to store heat and cooling (Trombe walls, stone, slate or masonry floors in front of south-facing glass).
6. Low wind profile in climates that have a greater heating season than cooling season.
7. Installation of proven energy-efficient appliances.
8. Open-floor plans that promote natural air movement and convection as well as better space utilization.
9. The use of indigenous material where applicable (pisé, native stone, cordwood, adobe).
10. The creation of earth-protected housing where applicable.
11. The installation of alternative energy systems, i.e., wind electric and solar photovoltaic cells, composting toilets, greenhouses, etc.
12. Terrascaping and landscaping that provide wind protection in the winter and shading in the summer.

Note: In hot climates solar orientation and glazing would be reversed to promote better cooling and heat protection.

Once these basic criteria are met, the rest will fall into place easily. Many "specialists" in the building industry consider the use of natural materials to be retrogressive and archaic. The very opposite is true. Attractive designs using these natural, on-site materials are numerous. Lack of familiarity with these materials and their utilization are the main reasons that builders are slow to accept them. We tend to fear the unknown and this is the reason that workshops to teach the use of these materials are necessary and should be included in the curriculum of every technical and community college.

If I were an aspiring young builder I would develop several house plans that utilized natural and recycled materials, cost them out and build them for sale as cheaply as possible. One would not get rich this way but I would rather be known as the builder of quality cheap houses than as a builder of prestige homes no one could afford.

The self-builder has a great deal more flexibility than the professional builder in choosing land, materials and being able to design for his own needs. The ability of the self-builder to take time and shop for recycled materials also reduces costs.

Often it appears that the human factor has been overlooked in mass-produced housing. The feelings that result from living in a home either result in a bond or indifference. It is this bond that makes the difference between being an occupant or having a personal attachment that adds to life's enjoyment.

A dwelling is a living organism with many facets. Those who merely occupy a space seldom sense the life of the structure. A home breathes due to air movement, both natural and induced, and even groans and creaks as we do. The groaning and creaking is the result of expansion and contraction of materials during a cycle of heating and cooling. It is therefore important that you help design the living structure that will surround, shelter and protect you. Your personality will intertwine with that of the structure and you will be more complete. The following chapters should give you the knowledge to build your own "Cheap Shelter" and breathe life into it.

2

Current Worldwide Indigenous Designs

The title of this chapter provides a large order to fill since the designs would be almost uncountable and the materials equally varied. What I will try to accomplish is to furnish an accounting of basic categories and materials. As mentioned earlier, shelter is a very personal means of expression and once you look outside of the Western technocratic culture, you will find that shelter variety abounds.

Many of America's early shelter designs were anchored in European tradition but were also influenced by such factors as material availability, labor shortages and the lack of skilled artisans. The enduring European distrust of and prejudice against frame construction carried over in the early use of logs and heavy timber-framed structures. Even today many European visitors to America are surprised by our predisposition for wooden houses. They wonder at the severe fire hazard, the general looseness and frailty of wood construction and the weakness of wood itself: It rots, bends, breaks, warps, burns, swells, shrinks and demands constant maintenance. Europeans cannot understand why we do not take advantage of stone, pisé, brick and other plentiful materials.

The general categories that most designs fall into are: Pole-supported buildings, post and beam, framed, compression or self-supporting and unframed wall systems that support various roof configurations. A breakdown of these terms is necessary at this point in order to fully understand how the designs are assembled and planned out.

Pole buildings are constructed by placing vertical poles into the ground to serve as supports for the roof and act as fastening members for the wall material. The main advantage to this type of structure is its inherent strength and simplicity. These dwellings are especially popular in areas of the world that are earthquake prone. Since each pole is independent of the others, the structure can move without a foundation to break up and cause the building to crumble.

Illus. 1 (Above left). Eighteen-foot rail-road yard or switch tie used as post for mechanical workshop support system. (Note the black poly plastic wrap around lower portion placed in the ground to protect it from rot.)

Illus. 2 (Above right). How posts are spaced to receive beams.

Illus. 3 (Left). Here you see beams in place to tie posts together and form the support system for the rafters.

Post-and-beam framing is sometimes combined with pole building. The posts can either be in the ground as the poles in a pole building or set on a post-supported deck or masonry foundation. The main advantages to post-and-beam framing are fast erection time, less materials and its strength. Post-and-beam framing has been used for centuries simply as a logical method, using the least material and labor. This method utilizes heavy timber posts spaced from six to twelve feet apart as vertical framing members. The horizontal pieces in turn are heavy beams that fasten the vertical posts together into a rigid framework. The

Illus. 4 (Above). Photo shows three-by-fourteens used in post-and-beam home as rafters on four-foot centers.

Illus. 5 (Below). Exterior of 4,600-square-foot post-and-beam home built on three levels. This house was built entirely from recycled materials for $20,000.

wide spacing between members is known as "bay spacing." Older houses had very wide spacing and used trees which were "squared off" with an adz. These trees were found on or near the building site, and due to its tremendous weight, a number of men were usually required to raise the frame after it was assembled.

19

Illus. 6. Telephone poles used as rafters on four-foot centers in the kitchen. These same poles extend to the exterior and support an outside balcony.

This may be one of the reasons that post-and-beam was replaced by lightweight framing techniques. Laminating three rough-sawn two-by-sixes together, creates a post that is lightweight but as strong as a heavy timber. This technique allows the use of rough-sawn lumber from local saw mills while avoiding the buying and transporting of planed dimensional lumber from the local lumber emporium at much higher prices.

Post-and-beam is simply a very strong frame that still needs to be filled in with a wall system. This filling can be applied to the outside of the frame or filled in between the frame members. In many of the older houses, the filling was mud

Illus. 7. Laminated post, three two-by-sixes glued and cross nailed.

(drive nails in at an angle)

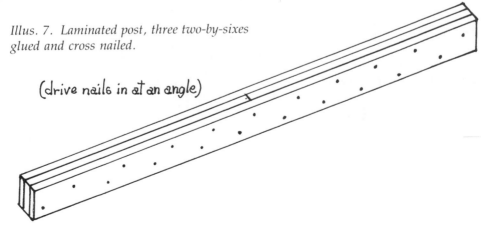

and daub, cordwood or stone. Modern post-and-beam homes have many other filler materials available, which will also add insulation to the structure. A more thorough discussion of materials occurs later in this chapter.

The massive dimensions of beams to span large open living areas while supporting the roof often limit the design flexibility of a structure. The lighter-weight beams made by laminating dimensional lumber still may not be strong enough to support the roof weight. Another fairly inexpensive solution to this problem is the laminated plywood boxbeam. These beams can be faced to resemble a laminated timber beam. The reason I mention this is because I originally considered using commercially produced laminated timber beams in one of my designs and immediately gave up the idea after pricing them. Also the three-to-six month delivery dates for the beams seemed inappropriate. A friend suggested making laminated plywood boxbeams. I read up on the techniques used in assembling these beams and was at once impressed with their relatively simple construction and strength. The light weight of the beams also make them very attractive to the self-builder with limited man power and equipment for lifting and placing heavy timber beams.

Laminated plywood boxbeams are fairly common in the construction field; therefore, specifications for span and load bearing are available from various plywood distributors. American Plywood Association in Chicago can furnish full details on fabrication. A curved plywood boxbeam will span twenty feet and give added strength as well as added dimensional perspective to a space. Flat ceilings can easily become boring, thus the use of the curved beams breaks this monotony and tends to distribute sound more evenly, making a room acoustically pleasant also. These beams can be made up by using a simple jig to bend the top and bottom pieces in the desired curve and then applying three-quarter-inch

Illus. 8. Nailed plywood and lumber beam. A section of 20-foot beam 24 inches deep will support 511 pounds per linear foot.

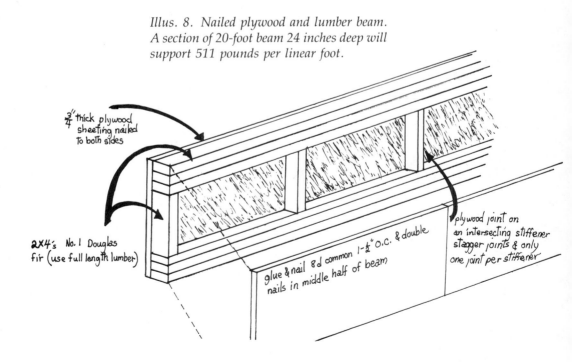

3/4" thick plywood sheeting nailed to both sides

2x4's No. 1 Douglas fir (use full length lumber)

glue & nail 8d common 1-1/2" o.c. & double nails in middle half of beam

plywood joint on an intersecting stiffener stagger joints & only one joint per stiffener

Plywood: APA RATED SHEATHING Exposure 1, marked PS 1 (see also item 3 in the Fabrication section for core gap restriction).

Lumber: 2 × 4 No. 1 Douglas fir or No. 1 KD15 southern pine (unless otherwise noted, reduce allowable loads by 19% for No.2 Douglas fir or No.2 KD15 southern pine).

Cross Sections

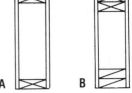

A   B

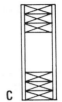

C

Tables are also based on the following:
Deflection: Less than 1/240 of span under total load.
Nailing: 8d common 1-1/2" o.c. each flange member (spacing may be doubled in middle half of beam).

ALLOWABLE LOAD[a] FOR 12"-DEEP ROOF BEAM OR HEADER (lb/lin ft)

Plywood	Cross-Section	Approx. Wt per Ft (lb)	10	12	14	16	18	20	22	24
1/2" 32/16	A	6	301*	251	199	153	121	98	81	68
1/2" 32/16	B	8	314*	262*	234*	196	174	148	122	103
3/4" 48/24	B	10	466*	388	302	231	183	148	122	103
3/4" 48/24	C	12	—	356*	305	260	205	166	138	116

ALLOWABLE LOAD[a] FOR 16"-DEEP ROOF BEAM OR HEADER (lb/lin ft)

Plywood	Cross-Section	Approx. Wt per Ft (lb)	10	12	14	16	18	20	22	24
1/2" 32/16	A	7	430*	358	284	218	172	139	115	97
1/2" 32/16	B	9	440*	367*	314*	275*	244	220	188	158
3/4" 48/24	B	11	650*	542	464	355	280	227	188	158
3/4" 48/24	C	14	—	506*	433*	379	337	275	228	191

ALLOWABLE LOAD[a] FOR 20"-DEEP ROOF BEAM OR HEADER (lb/lin ft)

Plywood	Cross-Section	Approx. Wt per Ft (lb)	10	12	14	16	18	20	22	24
1/2" 32/16	A	8	567*	474	370	283	224	181	150	126
1/2" 32/16	B	10	—	471*	404*	353*	314	283	255	214
3/4" 48/24	B	13	833*	694	595	482	381	309	255	214
3/4" 48/24	C	15	—	659*	565*	445*	440	391	324	272

ALLOWABLE LOAD[a] FOR 24"-DEEP ROOF BEAM OR HEADER (lb/lin ft)

Plywood	Cross-Section	Approx. Wt per Ft (lb)	10	12	14	16	18	20	22	24
1/2" 32/16	A	9	701*	584	456	349	276	223	184	155
1/2" 32/16	B	11	—	574*	492*	431*	383*	345	313	271
3/4" 48/24	B	14	1013*	844*	724	611	483	391	323	271
3/4" 48/24	C	17	—	—	697*	610*	542	488	422	355

(a) Includes 15% snow loading increase.
*Lumber may be No. 2 Douglas fir or No. 2 KD15 southern pine.

plywood side members. The increased design flexibility these members contribute make them a must for anyone contemplating post-and-beam construction.

The boxbeams can be laminated together with clear epoxy glue. I recommend that you use a commercial-grade adhesive instead of the hardware grade. There are an impressive array of adhesives manufactured for every purpose imaginable. While not cheap, this adhesive goes a long way and is incredibly strong. I even read about a concrete bridge that broke in two and was jacked up and bonded back together through the use of one of these adhesives.

Framing techniques utilized widely in the United States are commonly known, so I will not dwell on them only to list some of the advantages, disadvantages and suggested improvements on the system. Two-by-four framing was

Joint and Stiffener Layouts

developed as a standardized, mechanized means of construction that skilled craftsmen could utilize to mass-produce homes for an increasingly mobile and specialized society. It has been very successful at accomplishing this feat, but at what cost?

The costs go far beyond the lumber and labor costs. The real costs include depletion of our forests at a rate greater than replanting can accommodate. The vast amount of fossil fuel consumed in cutting, transporting, finishing and distributing dimensional lumber for framing also must be counted. The real detriment is the fact that few self-builders possess the necessary skills to properly assemble a framed structure. Framing also requires more material (wood) than other methods and makes ready kindling in case of fire. Two-by-four wall construction also limits the use of insulation and offers many areas of infiltration. As you can surmise, I am not a great fan of this building method. Since it is widely accepted and used, sometimes it is more easily altered than ended, so the following are suggestions that make the method more acceptable.

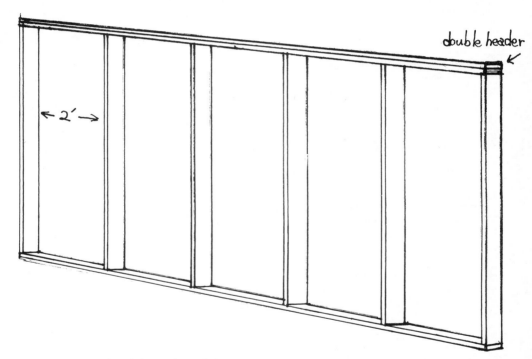

Illus. 9. Two-by-eight-inch wall frame with two-foot spacing and double top plate.

The use of two-by-eights or tens would allow wider spacing of the vertical wall-frame members. A minimum of six inches of insulation in the walls between these members would greatly increase the energy efficiency of the structure while allowing less infiltration and conduction. Siding a structure of this type with cypress plywood left to weather naturally would not only look nice but serve to brace this modified post-and-beam framed configuration. The use of construction adhesive to bond all members also would greatly increase strength while preventing infiltration. Laminating two members together for top and bottom plates on this wall would also add strength to this framing modification. The self-builder would do well to shop for used or recycled lumber. Many demolition firms allow subcontracts on components within a project. This provides cured, economic lumber with your sweat being the main ingredient.

Illus. 10. Frame construction, passive solar workshop that could easily be converted to a small two-storey home. Note the black-painted block interior wall used as heat sink.

Compression and self-supporting structures include all types of domed and arched designs. Any design that relies upon its own shape for structural support falls into this category. The geodesic dome that Fuller created is in this designation as are the mud-thatched beehive huts of Africa. The familiar Quonset hut of World War II vintage is another form of compression design. Umbrella tents, tunnel tents and other portable recreational shelters are either compression or tension designs, also. The main difference between these designs and all other designs is that in other designs a dead load of the roof is supported by either beams, rafters, or trusses on a separate wall system. The compression or tension design integrates the roof and wall.

Compression or tension designs can be either highly technical or extremely simple. The earliest excavations that were dug, using an arch shape for support were compression designs. The overburden of soil compressed the arch and kept the roof from collapsing. Many ancient societies shaped mud bricks into arches and domes for living purposes and food storage. Early burial vaults were arched designs. Geodesic domes are highly technical and require precise engineering for the proper angles used in the many interconnected pieces that make up the dome.

Illus. 11. Mud brick beehive hut.

A simple dome hut or home may be easily constructed by using mud brick or recycled masonry brick. All that is required is a center stake the height of the center of the structure and some string. An arc is swung from the center stake for each course of brick that is slightly less in diameter than the preceding one. The end result is a perfectly shaped dome with either a flue hole in the center or a skylight. Side windows of various shapes may also be incorporated by inserting support frames in the desired locations. The exterior may then be plastered if desired or coated with Surewall or a similar product for waterproofing. One of the problems associated with a dome or arch structure is that of insulating it. Rigid insulation will not conform to the shape, fibre insulation cannot be readily covered

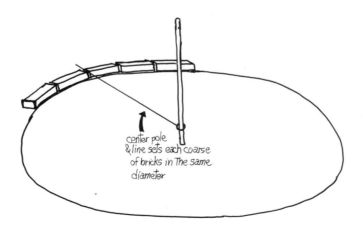

center pole
& line sets each coarse
of bricks in The same
diameter

Illus. 12. Center pole and line keeps everything straight.

and protected, so a sprayed-on polyurethane is about all that is left. A liquid protective covering of plaster would then have to be applied. Although the cost of spray-applied insulation is fairly high, the self-builder will not have the additional structural expenses usually present in other designs, so the overall costs should still be very low.

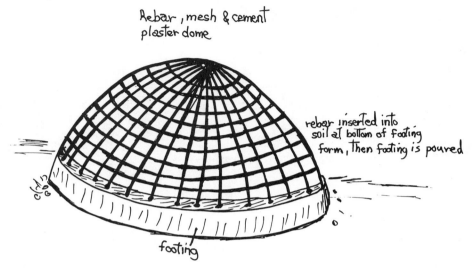

Rebar, mesh & cement plaster dome

rebar inserted into soil at bottom of footing form, then footing is poured

footing

Illus. 13. Rebar, mesh and cement plaster dome.

Other arches and domes that are simple for the self-builder to construct are those that use a network of recycled or leftover steel reinforcing bars and heavy mesh wire to form the arch or dome. This network is then plastered over with cement to a thickness of one or two inches, which forms a very strong shell that

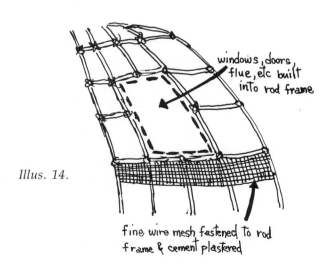

Illus. 14.

windows, doors, flue, etc built into rod frame

fine wire mesh fastened to rod frame & cement plastered

can be used as a surface structure or an underground mode. Again insulation presents the same problem previously mentioned. The clear-span space these designs provide is also very attractive since load-bearing support walls that diminish interior space in most buildings are not needed. This also means that as the family grows older and space requirements change, interior dividing walls can easily be moved to open up areas or enclose others.

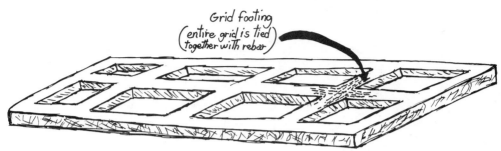

Illus. 15. Grid footing.

Non-framed wall systems are those that support the roof structure without the benefit of additional bracing from posts, beams or framing members. These walls are usually very massive and built out of concrete, rammed earth, cordwood or stone. As with any system, there are advantages and disadvantages. An obvious advantage is the lack of framing which cuts material and cost. Also a wall of this nature built from natural materials found on or near the building site has tremendous economy when compared with other systems. The added benefit of construction without the use of skilled labor also cuts the cost.

The main disadvantage is the fact that these wall systems are really just an extension of the footing; thus, if the footing fails, so does the wall, the roof, the building. It is therefore imperative that the footings be adequately designed to withstand the loads imposed on them. Any settling that occurs must be transmitted to the entire footing without any separation. This means that an extensive grid pattern should be designed to provide a large footprint on the ground when building on an expansive soil. The entire grid should all be tied together with adequate reinforcing steel bars to keep any one part of the grid from breaking away.

Load-bearing walls built from such natural materials as cordwood, stone and rammed earth cannot be stiffened through the use of reinforcing steel bars as in the case of concrete. The walls get their strength from their great mass and weight. Below grade these walls would not be able to withstand the lateral and vertical shear pressure of the earth if constructed as straight walls.

Any wall built below grade from these natural materials would have to get its strength from its shape. Either a circle or uniform curve anchored at both ends would be required to maintain the structural integrity of this type of wall system. There is the assumption on the part of many official agencies dealing with codes and permits that the use of supporting wall structural systems is unsafe, especially when constructed out of natural materials such as cordwood, fieldstone, and rammed earth. Not only is this assumption incorrect, it also has no basis in fact. If the footings or base upon which these walls stand is sound, the wall will be much stronger than a two-by-four framed wall and certainly last much longer.

This is supported by the fact that many of the buildings in Europe and other places are made from these natural or available materials and are standing after centuries of use.

Looking at the four basic structural categories from the standpoint of the entire environment in which the building will be constructed, each facet of that environment must be weighed to choose the category best suited. I feel very strongly that everyone should participate in the design of their own home if possible, and utilize natural materials available near or on site in its construction. This not only reduces material, transportation and labor costs but also reduces the demands placed on our environment and natural resources. The use of as many recycled materials as possible also contributes towards this goal. With this in mind, I have compiled the following list of questions that should be considered when deciding which category of structure to build, as well as what type of design to use.

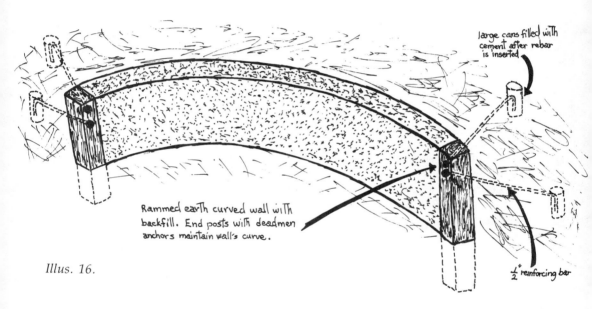

large cans filled with cement after rebar is inserted

Rammed earth curved wall with backfill. End posts with deadmen anchors maintain wall's curve.

Illus. 16.

½" reinforcing bar

Structural Categories and Design Considerations

1. Is the building site rural or urban?
2. What limiting socioeconomic conditions exist? (Examples are code restrictions, personal life-style choice as it affects building design, and the local population.)
3. Will you act as the builder, or will you subcontract the work?
4. What labor force is available to you and at what cost?
5. What natural materials are available on or near the building site?
6. What usable recycled materials are available within economic transport range?
7. If a mortgage is necessary, will the local lending institutions lend money on the type of structure you are planning?
8. What is the climate?
9. Will there be more heating days than cooling days?

10. Will a below grade structure work better in this climate and site, or should a surface structure be considered?

11. Is the proposed design adaptable to change in space usage over a protracted time as family needs change?

12. Is the site suited for passive solar design principles?

13. Are there laws protecting your site's sun rights?

14. Have the various needs of family members been considered? (These include proximity to work, school, shopping, recreation, etc.)

15. What will the maintenance factors be for the proposed structure once it is occupied?

16. What are the topographical features of the site? (Sloped or flat? Soil type and subsoil conditions? Expansive or stable soil? What are drainage conditions, flooding conditions, erosion probabilities, slope shift possibilities? Is it near a fault or other natural hazard? What is the hydraulic condition of site?)

17. Do the site conditions lend themselves to a building constructed as a pole structure, on pilings, slab or footings?

18. Should a pole, post-and-beam, tension or compression, framed, or a supporting wall structure be considered for the site?

19. Compare cost and time factors acting as a self-builder, getting a subcontractor or retaining a contractor to be responsible for entire project.

20. Who will buy the house if it becomes necessary to move? (The resale potential influences lending institutions greatly.)

I am including a checklist of passive solar design criteria that should be a part of every design and structural category. This list will help determine the design once the structural category has been decided. The remaining chapters deal with specific designs and construction techniques using various natural materials, recycled materials and conversions of various existing structures for habitation. This solar checklist is applicable to each and every design concept found in these chapters.

Passive Solar Checklist
1. Orient the structure towards either solar gain or protection, depending on climatic conditions.

2. Use extensive glazing on south side of structure for heat gain in cold climate.

3. Limit glazing on west and north sides of structure in cold climate.

4. If possible, apply insulation to outside of any masonry or concrete structure so structural mass can store heat. Protect insulation with plaster or other sheeting.

5. Isolate as much mass as possible inside structure to retain heat and coolant as a carryover for occupants.

6. Keep floor plan as open as possible to allow convection airflow and thus eliminate duct work.

7. Surface structures should incorporate movable insulation to cover glazing at night in winter to avoid heat loss due to conduction.

8. Provide massive insulation of walls and ceiling as well as under floors.

9. Limit wind profile. (Underground is best, bermed second and a single story protected by plantings is third in efficiency.)

10. Berms, bumps, and bushes protect as well as deciduous trees for south-sun protection in summer and evergreens for winter wind protection on the west and north of structure.

NOTE: Insulation should be dictated by climate.

3

Potpourri

As stated at the beginning, shelter should be a personal expression. For some with an extra ingredient of whimsy in their natures, shelter can take on many forms and guises. I have seen rail cars, water towers, wine barrels, barns, schoolhouses and barges converted into fanciful dwellings. Almost anything large enough to hold a few people can be converted into a habitat. Many times it seems that the sameness of everything in our modern society is designed to strangle any form of individuality. Even our laws prohibit any extreme in personal shelter expression. Neighborhood covenants disallow any structure that does not "fit in." This means that a structure must be in keeping with the general design trend of the neighborhood, as well as containing a minimal number of square feet of floor space with an attendant cost structure. In other words, keep the poor and the rich separate.

A variance in the building codes for your area may be the only way to either build or convert a structure that is not a frame building with windows, exits, stairs and minimal square feet of floor space. This is probably a good place to discuss codes and how to live with or without them. First of all, presume that the people in the codes and permits section of your city or county office are there to help. Most of these people are knowledgeable about various forms of construction and can be of great assistance. If the existing code structure is so limiting that the person in charge of issuing building permits cannot issue one for your design or conversion, it may be necessary to request a variance. A variance can be issued for special-purpose structures, experimental buildings or any singular design that the granter of permits feels may have merit. Variances can also be granted for various parts of a structure that do not meet a particular code definition. If the person you are dealing with doesn't feel that he or she can issue you a variance, then you may have to resort to the "Report." This is a system that I have devised over the years to deal with bureaucracies. The system seldom fails if followed religiously.

The "Report" system plays on the fact that few bureaucrats like to sign their name to anything that is not a standard form issued by their department. Start at the bottom of the bureaucratic line and deal with the appropriate individual. Take a pad of paper and a pencil with you. Record the date, time, the person's name and the essence of the conversation as to why or why not that individual says a variance cannot be granted. Also include your reasoning as to why it should be granted, then request that individual read your report and sign it as to its accuracy so that you may then get an appointment with that individual's superior. It is often at that point that the person decides to grant the variance rather than sign your report and make an appointment for you with his or her boss. Continue this method on up the ladder until you reach the top. Usually your variance will be granted before the second person is seen. This presumes that your design or conversion is basically sound and not life-threatening in any manner. Do not act haughty. Act the part of the good citizen needing help.

Should you be turned down on the variance, it may then be necessary to resort to action that is still within the law, but not necessarily the intent of the law. For instance, the law says that anything less than twenty acres in the country may not be built on. Essentially twenty acres is considered a farm and a farmer can build on that land without a permit in most areas. If you could get three others who wanted five acres apiece but could not afford to buy twenty acres each, you could form a corporation and buy the twenty acres as a group. You still could not legally subdivide the land to build on five-acre plots, but since a corporation is considered legally to be an individual, it can own the land for all individuals with attendant tax breaks. Each individual would then be issued stock for the equivalent value of their home and portion of the twenty acres. Everyone could then build and simply sell their stock when they wished to sell or move. Getting an area zoned for special use, then buying land in that area is another way of getting a permit for an unusual structure. As I said, these are methods that are within the law, but basically abrogate it. It is always good to retain an attorney to verify that you are still within the law for your area.

Many times it is necessary to break the law in order to get it changed. If you break a law in order to have that law tested in a court of law, you should be willing also to live with the results if that law is upheld. If you have the time and patience, laws can be changed by going through appropriate channels. This usually requires the hiring of an attorney to draw up an amendment to the code, then the circulation of a petition illustrating public desire for the change. The amendment then will be scheduled for a public hearing before the appropriate governing body (usually the city council or county board). Any changes recommended at that time will have to be included in the amendment. The amendment will then be scheduled for another hearing and vote. If it passes, the code has been effectively changed for the benefit of everyone. This process usually takes anywhere from one to two years, so as I said—you have to have time and patience.

You may also elect to just build without notifying anyone and hope that you won't get caught. It used to be fairly easy to do that, but now there are so many government employees at various levels that report to each other, it is nearly impossible not to get caught. If you are caught, your penalty may be a slap on the wrist, a fine or the condemnation of the building with its attendant demolition. As a summation, let me just say that I do not advocate the breaking of the law unless there is absolutely no other way. If you do break the law, you must be willing to pay the price. If enough people voice the need for change in the codes and make relevant suggestions to the appropriate sources, they will get changed. Petitions signed by many voters never fail to influence elected officials.

Moving along to the subject at hand: conversions of structures for habitation, a real assessment should be made as to the economic and structural feasibility of the proposed project. Many people have read books such as *Woodstock Handmade Houses, Rescued Buildings*, and *Renegade Houses*.* These books depict very colorful and attractive conversions that inspire many people to copy this life-style.

Emulating someone else's project is not all bad since you can learn from their mistakes, but it also has a cost. That cost may be more labor and materials than if you designed and built an economic design from scratch. The uniqueness of the project being considered may make it worth the cost, however, especially if it enhances your creative instincts.

Finding a structure that fits your fancy and has potential for conversion may be more difficult than appears on the surface. Although there are thousands of unused and abandoned structures throughout our country, many of them may be unsuitable for any conversion attempt. The underpinnings of any structure should be carefully examined. The life of the building and its occupants literally stand or fall on these supports. Next, check posts and beams, rafters and any exposed support member for rot or insect infestation. The roof rafters and sheeting should be solid even if the roofing is in need of repair. Since the aforementioned are the ingredients for any sound building, these essentials should be intact. The shell of a building is half of its completed cost. The interior finish makes up the other half. Therefore, if one hopes to reap a financial benefit by converting an existing structure, it must be structurally strong.

Once a structure is located that seems to fit your requirements, check on zoning laws and codes that restrict getting a building permit for converting the structure for occupancy. If permits can be obtained, then the real job may be getting the owner to sell at a reasonable price. Many abandoned or unused buildings are owned by absentee landlords. These properties in many cases are left as tax deductions without any intent to fix them up or use them. An owner may also assume that simply because you are interested in converting the structure, it is now worth more money and will quote a price that is unrealistic. It is best not to be overeager in your approach. Check on the property tax value listed for that property and make an offer in accordance.

The following checklist will help with the initial inspection of the structure.

1. What type of structure is it? (Post-and-beam, frame, tension, supporting wall, pole, etc?)

2. What type of underpinnings? (Footings, basement, pole, pilings, slab, etc?)

3. How durable are those underpinnings and will they withstand the modifications you intend for the structure?

4. Are the basic supporting members solid and will they take the increased loads of the modifications proposed?

*Robert Haney and David Ballantine, *Woodstock Handmade Houses*, Ballantine Publishing. Roland Jacopetti and Ben VanMeter, *Rescued Buildings*, Santa Barbara, CA: Capra Press, 1977. Eric Hoffman, *Renegade Houses*, Running Press.

5. Will increased fire protection need to be designed into the structure?

6. Can the structure be thoroughly insulated without extensive modifications to the shell?

7. Is the present wiring adequate and safe or will the structure need to be rewired?

8. Is there plumbing in the structure and how much modification to it will be needed for habitation?

9. Is the structure suited to passive solar modification based upon the criteria listed earlier?

10. What recycled materials are available near the structure that can be used in the conversion?

11. Will the utility bills be within reason when the conversion is complete?

12. Can the recycled building be sold for enough to cover the cost of conversion should you have to move?

Illus. 17–31 depict the variety of possibilities that are available to the person with imagination and the guts to buck tradition.

I have also included photos of two structures that have conversion possibilities. An accompanying drawing illustrates the modifications that I would make to render one of these structures both habitable and visually attractive (Illus. 32, 33, 34).

Illus. 17. A garage that has been converted into an attractive commercial woodworking shop through the use of a bay window and other windows used for solar gain on the south.

Illus. 18 (Above). This house was purchased for next to nothing, moved to the site and renovated. The cost for renovation was mostly sweat. The siding is the old weathered boarding removed, turned over and nailed back on at an angle instead of horizontally.

Illus. 19 (Left). Looking out from the inside through the greenhouse used for winter gardening.

Illus. 20. The same exterior siding shown in Illus. 18 is used here for an unusual ceiling.

Illus. 21. The generous use of sky-lights provides additional heat and a cheery interior.

Illus. 22. Turn-of-the-century wooden railroad caboose is used as a home by an elderly woman whose husband had worked on the railroad.

Illus. 23. Though relatively small, the interior space is light and open.

Illus. 24. Note the beautiful craftsmanship of the wood-beamed ceiling.

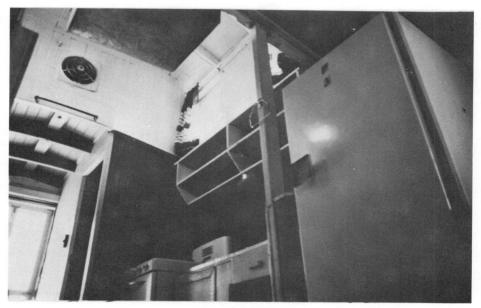

Illus. 25. The raised windows make good clerestory windows. Note also the exhaust fan in the raised area, an excellent venting location above the stove in the kitchen below.

Illus. 26. Stone carriage house and stable converted into handsome home.

Illus. 27. Older two-storey home renovated through the use of recycled materials. Note the greenhouse made from discarded storm windows, and the attractive balcony.

Illus. 28. How the recycled storm windows were assembled for an attractive greenhouse.

Illus. 29. Another older home renovated for energy efficiency. Greenhouses like this not only add heat but are wonderful places to sit.

Illus. 30 Greenhouse and added cement-block chimney for an airtight woodburning stove.

Illus. 31. Old stable and carriage house, turned garage, now turned into small home. Under renovation at present, it will have a large expanse of south-facing glass in upper dormer for heat gain.

Illus. 32 (Above). Country school that could easily be converted into attractive rural living space.

Illus. 33 (Right). Water tower that I have proposed for a two-storey home conversion shown in Illus. 34.

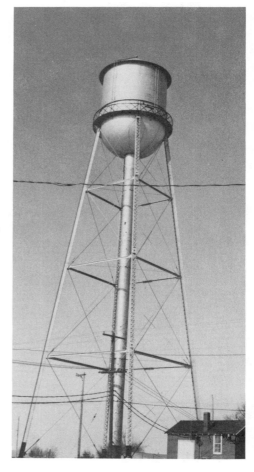

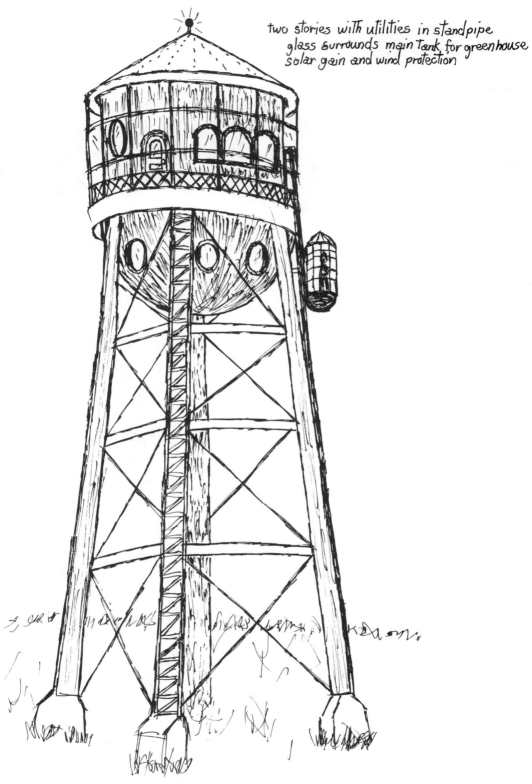

two stories with utilities in standpipe
glass surrounds main tank for greenhouse
solar gain and wind protection

Illus. 34. Water tower home with outside elevator.

44

4

Dirt Designs: Pisé, Rammed Earth, and Pounded Ground

Some of the most exciting developments in the design and construction of dwellings for the future utilize one of the earliest materials used by man—dirt. This exciting new/old medium offers tremendous advantages when coupled with modern construction and design technology. There are many ways to use earth in the construction of a dwelling, but this chapter will cover "rammed earth," or pisé, techniques. The art of pounding ground into solid shapes dates back to the Assyrians and Babylonians. A large portion of the Great Wall of China is rammed earth. Our own government became interested in rammed earth during the Great Depression. Federally funded rammed earth housing was created for the homeless in Alabama during the 1930's. The project was supervised by architect Thomas Hibben. Many of those homes are still standing. There are apartments in France that predate World War I that are still being used today. The point is that pisé, or rammed earth, is still a most viable material and technique for constructing modern energy-efficient dwellings.

The West tends to become enamored with new technology and techniques while forgetting timeless appropriate technology that is both durable and efficient. The capital-intensive quest for ever newer and more exotic synthetic building materials has put the cost of a modest-sized new home out of reach for most of those needing shelter.

A definition of what rammed earth is and is not would be appropriate at this point. Many people think of any earth-constructed home as either adobe or perhaps some form of sod. It is neither. Adobe is essentially just dried mud in brick form. Sod is the topsoil held together by a network of roots and cut into slabs. Rammed earth is the subsoil (usually clay and sand) that is pulverized and compacted into a sturdy form. The ideal soil mix is seventy percent sand and thirty percent clay. This mix with the correct amount of moisture packs into a solid

45

mass as durable as sandstone. The compaction causes a chemical change in the mixture. Colloids (Gk. *kolla* glue) in the soil bond and become solid as stone. Colloid in physics is a substance composed of particles that are extremely small but larger than most molecules. Colloids do not actually dissolve, but remain suspended in a suitable gas, liquid or solid.

It is this unique change that takes place during compaction that gives pisé its strength and beauty. Most of my students are very skeptical that dirt can become as stone until they actually tamp a test block. Once the steel tamper begins to ring as it strikes the block they can both hear and feel its hardness. The real appeal seems to be the fact that the student is actually creating something out of such a mundane substance as soil. It is during the actual process of construction that most of the students gain their enthusiasm for this ancient building art.

An evaluation of the weaknesses and strengths of pisé may help you decide if this is the construction medium for you. Every construction method and material has its weaknesses as well as strengths and it is this honest appraisal that will allow you to adapt your personality and skills to the task without becoming unduly discouraged.

Pisé, or rammed earth, allows you to trade your sweat instead of your cash. This is basically a labor-intensive construction method as opposed to a capital-intensive one. Since the soil is found on site, the cost of material is eliminated for the most part (sand may have to be brought in), as well as transportation costs. If one uses hand tools only, ramming earth is very heavy work and requires stamina. Limited mechanization greatly reduces both the labor and time factor but again raises costs somewhat. It is this heavy labor that scares most people off. Later in the chapter I will show how to greatly reduce this element.

The plus side of the ledger is more weighty and I think worth serious consideration. As mentioned, the material is available on site. No technical skills are required to use this material, so even if it is necessary to hire labor to complete the project, unskilled labor can be hired at less cost than skilled. The tools needed to work the soil are simple and available at any hardware dealer's. The forms can also be built with little carpentry skill. Combining rammed earth with modern design principles gives strength even in earthquake areas. The structure requires little to no interior finish work, thus eliminating another major cost factor. The wiring and receptacles can be incorporated into the wall system directly. No carcinogenic properties are incorporated in this system. The structure has great mass for strength and to maintain an even internal temperature. The system goes a long way in helping to stem the damaging consequences that arise from the pilfering of our natural resources to build frame structures. Rammed earth walls are fireproof, dry, rotproof, soundproof and are fantastic solar collectors. I am an enthusiast of rammed earth for both surface and underground homes. A properly designed rammed-earth home can be built for twenty percent to fifty percent less than an equivalent frame structure.

If you feel now that this is your medium, the remaining portion of the chapter will tell you how to go about constructing a rammed-earth home and give you some design concepts that you may feel free to enlarge upon.

Site preparation is the first and most important aspect of the proposed structure. A site that allows you to make the most of this medium is very important. Find a site that provides a wide sun exposure so that you can utilize rammed earth's thermal storage capabilities during winter months. Due to its great mass, very substantial footings are required for rammed earth. If the design is to be a surface one, try to choose a site that provides some natural thermal protection against cold winter north and west winds. If excavation is necessary, try to disturb the surrounding eco-structure as little as possible. Also, if fill is required, do the compaction slowly and methodically to lessen the possibility of settling. Design and plan the footings with a lip to help fasten the forms in place. Be sure the site drains well to avoid the possibility of running or standing water against the walls.

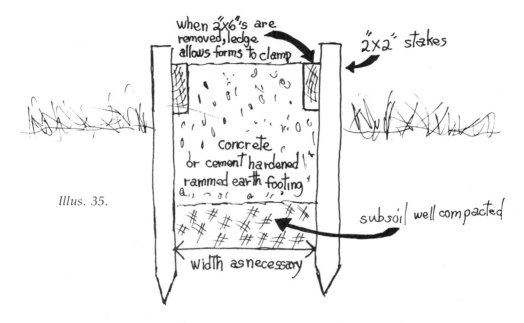

Illus. 35.

Prior to pouring the footings, it will be necessary to stockpile enough subsoil to ram for the wall system. Scrape the site with a tractor. Pile the topsoil separately for later use on the roof as a base to lay sod on. Clay or subsoil only should be used for wall material. Topsoil is too full of organic material such as roots and will not pack well. Usually six inches of soil scraped from the site will be adequate for the walls. Six inches scraped from a thirty-by-forty foot space will yield twenty-two cubic yards of compaction soil. Remember, six inches of soil poured into the form will pack into three inches of wall. Your site should be flat and allow enough room for a small tractor with a front-end loader to maneuvre, otherwise you will have to lift dirt to the top of the forms by hand.

A proper soil mix is essential in order to obtain the optimum compaction in the form. A soil analysis can be performed by a soil engineer, however this is really not necessary since all that is needed is a ratio of thirty percent clay to seventy percent sand. Various subsoils will have their own peculiarities and some will compact more quickly than others. A very simple test that will show how much sand and how much clay is in a given subsoil can be performed by simply mulching up two cups of soil and putting them into a quart jar. Fill the rest of the jar with water and shake it until all of the soil particles are suspended in the solution. Let the jar sit overnight. A visible line should appear between the soil and sand. Remember, do not use topsoil in the test since it is too full of organic material to give you the formation that you need. Roughly three-quarters of the mix should be sand with the remainder being clay.

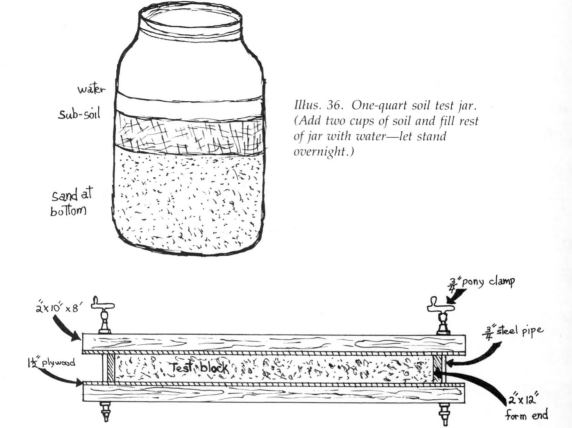

water
Sub-soil

Illus. 36. One-quart soil test jar. (Add two cups of soil and fill rest of jar with water—let stand overnight.)

sand at bottom

¾" pony clamp

2"x10" x 8'

¾" steel pipe

1½" plywood

Test block

2"x 12"
form end

Illus. 37. Top view of pony clamp form for ramming test block.

After determining the subsoil mix and deciding how much, if any, sand will have to be added, form a test block to see how the mix will compact. I have rammed a number of mixtures over the years and each soil will compact different-ly. You will sense when the mix is right by the solid ring it will have when fully compacted and the hand ram is dropped. The correct amount of moisture is also very important. A mix that is too wet will never compact into a solid, and one that is too dry will not have enough cohesion to stay together. A very simple test can be performed on a continual basis as the work is in progress to check on moisture content. Simply take a handful of soil mix and squeeze it into a ball. If the soil stays in a ball and then shatters when dropped on a hard surface, the mix is just right. If it splatters when dropped, it is too wet. If it will not stay in a ball when squeezed, it is too dry. Elementary, my dear Watson.

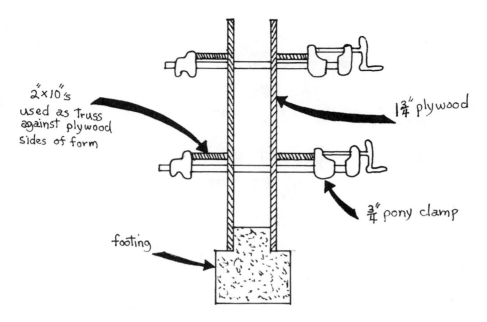

2"x10"s used as Truss against plywood Sides of form

1¾" plywood

¾" pony clamp

footing

Illus. 38. End view of pony clamp form for ramming test block.

A wall that is strictly sand and clay is very durable and quite strong, but due to code restrictions in your area it may be desirable to add some portland cement to the mix. A very small amount of cement added to the mix increases the strength factor many times over. As little as five percent cement added to the mixture will increase the strength factor of the wall about five hundred percent. This is an intelligent use of cement. The small added cost for the cement is more than offset by the benefit.

There are a couple of ways to prepare soil for compaction. A small cement mixer works quite well for mixing sand and water with the pulverized clay that has been stockpiled. The mix can also be "eyeballed" as it is being stockpiled and the sand mixed in with the rototiller. This requires a very reliable crew. I prefer the cement mixer approach for the best consistency. I like the idea of utilizing natural and recycled materials to construct a shelter, but I am not a total purist when it comes to back-breaking labor. Anyone seriously contemplating the construction of a rammed-earth home would do well to barter for the use of a tractor with a scraper blade on the rear and a front-end loader along with a cement mixer and either a pneumatic tamper or a "Whacker Packer" which is a mechanized tamper run by a small two-cycle chainsaw engine. These tools fall into the appropriate technology category and certainly reduce the physical labor requirements to reasonable proportions.

Forms are the next concern. Needless to say, they have to be strong. Up to twenty-two thousand pounds per square foot is exerted on the sides of the forms as the soil is rammed. David and Lydia Miller have built several rammed-earth homes over the years and have taught seminars at *Mother Earth News* on the subject. They prefer complete wall forms built out of thick plywood and two-by-

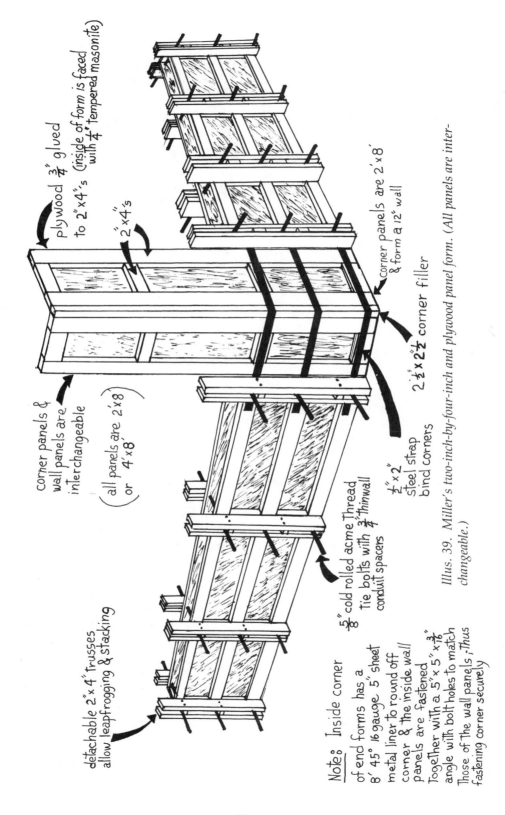

plywood 3/4" glued to 2"x4"'s (inside of form is faced with 1/4" tempered masonite)

2"x4"'s

corner panels are 2'x8' & form a 12" wall

2 1/2" x 2 1/2" corner filler

corner panels & wall panels are interchangeable

(all panels are 2'x8' or 4'x8')

1/4" x 2" steel strap bind corners

5/8" cold rolled acme Thread Tie bolts with 3/4" thinwall conduit spacers

detachable 2"x4" trusses allow leapfrogging & stacking

Note: Inside corner of end forms has a 8' 45° 16 gauge 5" sheet metal liner to round off corner & the inside wall panels are fastened Together with a 5"x5"x3/16" angle with bolt holes to match Those of the wall panels. Thus fastening corner securely.

Illus. 39. Miller's two-inch-by-four-inch and plywood panel form. (All panels are interchangeable.)

50

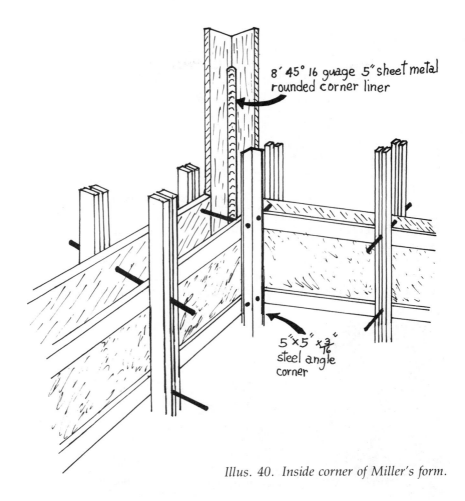

8' 45° 16 guage 5" sheet metal rounded corner liner

5"x5"x3/16" steel angle corner

Illus. 40. Inside corner of Miller's form.

four reinforcing. These forms are held together with numerous heavy bolts extending through the rammed soil. These bolts have to be removed once the wall is rammed. The forms are massive and very heavy to handle, set up and haul. The entire set of walls are formed, very similar to pouring a wall system. The advantage to this system is that it allows the work to progress rapidly once the forms are in place.

David Easton, a young architect-builder living in California, has developed a building system utilizing poured concrete footings, posts, bond beams and rammed earth filler wall sections. This system was developed to meet the stringent building codes in earthquake-prone California. His system has met code requirements in California, Kansas and Colorado. Since his walls are self-finishing, his structures still cost considerably less than other designs using conventional materials and techniques. While his system is very strong, it is also far more costly than necessary. All the added strength is for the benefit of the codes people, not for the safety of the structure.

A well-designed, rammed-earth home built on an integrated, reinforced footing is not likely to fall down in the first wind or tremor. It is my opinion that as

51

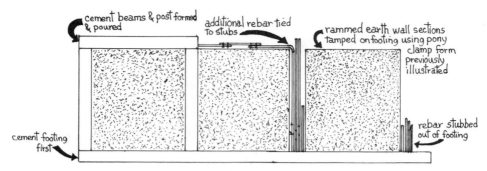

Illus. 41. David Easton's rammed-earth system.

long as the footings remain intact, the walls will also. Easton's top bond beam and supporting posts with reinforcing steel are essentially the framework of the structure and the rammed earth serves only the purpose of filling the space in between. A rammed-earth supporting wall system with some concrete in the mix will support the compression load of any roof design without the posts or bond

Illus. 42. Exterior and interior views of shell of old rammed-earth house. The upper roof structure used framing as well as lower walls. The exterior shows the rammed earth between the uprights and siding nailed over to protect earth fill.

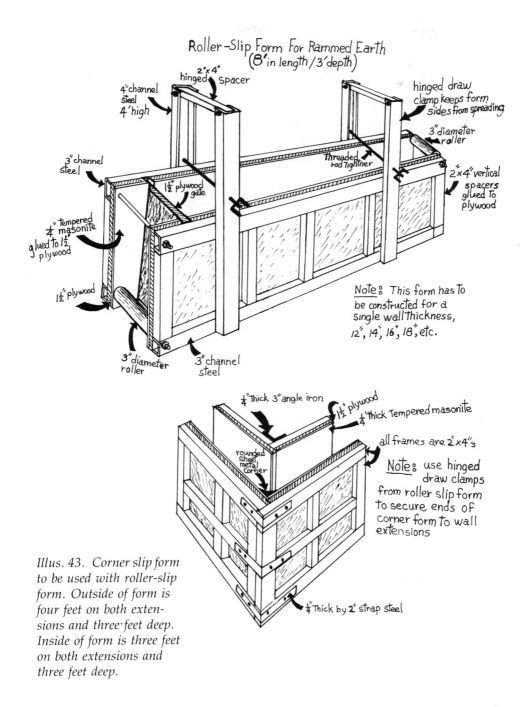

Roller-Slip Form For Rammed Earth
(8' in length / 3' depth)

4" channel steel 4' high

2"x4" hinged spacer

hinged draw clamp keeps form sides from spreading

3" diameter roller

3" channel steel

Threaded rod Tightner

2"x4" vertical spacers glued to plywood

1½" plywood gate

¼" tempered masonite glued to 1½" plywood

1½" plywood

Note: This form has to be constructed for a single wall thickness, 12", 14", 16", 18", etc.

3" diameter roller

3" channel steel

¼" thick 3" angle iron

1½" plywood

¼" thick Tempered masonite

rounded sheet metal corner

all frames are 2"x4"'s

Note: use hinged draw clamps from roller slip form to secure ends of corner form to wall extensions

¼" thick by 2" strap steel

Illus. 43. Corner slip form to be used with roller-slip form. Outside of form is four feet on both extensions and three feet deep. Inside of form is three feet on both extensions and three feet deep.

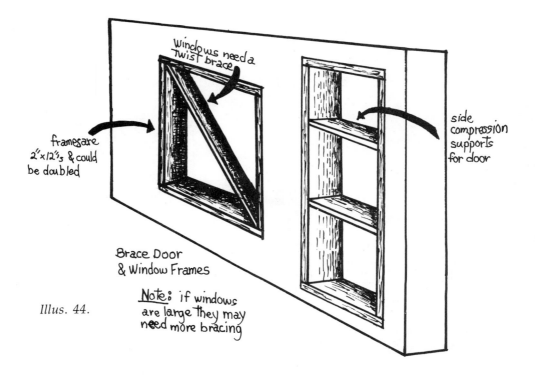

Windows need a Twist brace

side compression supports for door

frames are 2"x12"s & could be doubled

Brace Door & Window Frames

Illus. 44.

Note: if windows are large they may need more bracing

beams. I will give Mr. Easton all the credit in the world for getting the codes and permits people to think of other construction besides sticks and poured concrete.

Illus. 43 shows a slip-form that I have altered to assist the individual who wants to do most of the work himself without the benefit of a crew. This rather simple slip-form can be used to build round or semicircular structures as well as square or rectangular ones. The main advantage to this form is that it is relatively compact and can be handled by one person. The form allows the wall to be self-aligning and the forms can be loosened and rolled forward by simply turning a couple of wing nuts. The wall is also free of bolt holes. The only additional form that is needed is a corner form when doing square or rectangular structures. The corner form prevents a cold-joint at that point and, therefore, makes a stronger structure.

The entire wall system should be kept moist until completed so that each lift of dirt that is compacted on the layer below will bond with it. Wet burlap or other saturated material can be draped over the walls and covered with plastic. This will help prevent the moisture from evaporating too quickly. One additional advantage to Easton's post-and-beam system is that each rammed-earth wall section can be easily completed before moving on to the next one and therefore it will not be necessary to keep them wet.

Unlike concrete, the forms on rammed earth can be moved just as soon as that section is complete. Although the material will still be wet, and it will take several days for the surface to cure, it will be solid. It is a good idea to protect the walls for at least a week by covering them with plastic. This will prevent rain from eroding the soft surface. The footings should be high enough to also remove the wall from

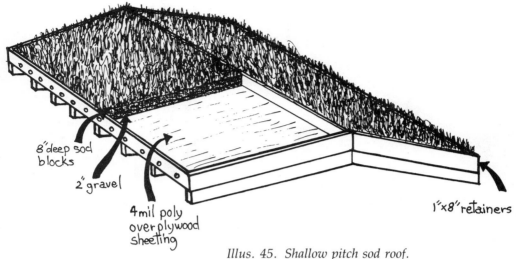

8" deep sod blocks

2" gravel

4mil poly over plywood sheeting

1"x8" retainers

Illus. 45. Shallow pitch sod roof.

roof shows layers of material/plywood over rafters, black poly, 2" gravel, 8" sod blocks, pressure treated retainer boards with 1" drain holes

ine threat of ground water and a good overhang should be designed to keep driving rain off of the walls.

Wiring can easily be incorporated into a rammed-earth wall by placing a conduit in the form and ramming earth around it. Care will have to be taken to avoid crushing the conduit and all outlet boxes should be blocked to avoid crushing. Windows and doors are also easy to install. The frames can be built from two-by-fours and filled around. Again it will be necessary to brace the frames as shown in Illus. 44 to avoid bowing or twisting from the compaction process.

Floors and roofs are also something that should be dealt with at this point. The roof not only keeps the weather off your head, but it is also a valuable tool for helping to move air through the house and to vent heat. The roof can add greatly to the beauty and grace of the living space if properly designed. Due to the desire to hold costs down, compromises are often made in building the roof. The roof is more than its shingles. Exposed rafters, beams and trusses can add to the interior beauty. I personally like exposed support systems, with a double roof incorporating twelve inches of insulation.

I also like sod roofs, even on surface structures. This goes for structures other than rammed, also. There are several advantages to sod roofs. Properly done, the sod roof is permanent and nearly impervious to high winds, hail and ultraviolet light which erode most other composite roofing materials. The thing I like most about sod roofing is the fact that it adds oxygen back to the atmosphere instead of reducing the green space of our cities. A sod roof does not have to have two feet of soil on it with the attendant massive support system. Six to eight inches of humus soil beneath a standard sod layer is more than adequate to maintain the sod and

Illus. 46. Miller's house built in 1945, with eighteen-inch rammed-earth walls. The south-facing sun room provides generous solar gain for cold weather.

provide the aforementioned benefits. The unorthodox appearance may attract unwanted attention for a spell, but once your neighbors see the benefits and the natural beauty of the grass, everyone will have to have one. The roof weight will be somewhere around seventy-five pounds per square foot. Either a shed roof or shallow-sloped A configuration will allow the use of sod.

If a more conventional roof is used, I would advise against using wooden shingles. They are not only expensive, but a fire hazard as well. High winds tend to blow any type of shingle off. The older the roof becomes, the more roof dandruff you will find in your yard afterward. The most economic and secure conventional roofing material is asphalt roll roofing. This material can be easily applied by the novice and is more durable in high winds than any shingle. A good choice would be a matching earth tone that complements the soft beige of the rammed-earth walls. (I also prefer nonplastered rammed earth.) This blending of color will keep the less attractive roll roofing from becoming the focal point of the exterior.

Remember that any house should be an integrated structure with all aspects of the construction blended into an agreeable habitat. It is excellent to acquire knowledge in various construction technologies, but do not use this knowledge just for the sake of "show." In the case of pisé, or rammed earth, utilize the basic passive solar technology previously listed along with good design principles before deciding that rammed earth is the particular material to use in your design. Most of the natural and recycled materials listed in these chapters can be integrated into almost any design complement that will fit your particular needs. Perhaps a blending of several natural materials and techniques into an integrated design that fits your personality would be most appropriate. Here again, let common sense prevail. Illus. 46−53 on the following pages demonstrate the fact that an earth home does not have to look like a Prairie Soddy. The Millers have contributed to the modern use of this appropriate technology more than anyone else I know and deserve much praise for their persistence.

Illus. 47. Second rammed-earth home built by the Millers in 1946. Note the generous use of south-facing glass for solar gain.

Illus. 48. View of Miller's rammed-earth home completed in 1950 in Colorado. Rammed-earth housing can be as modern and as attractive as any framed home.

Illus. 49. Closeup view shows mass of wall.

Illus. 50 (Below). Barn of rammed earth that was converted into a home in 1950.

Illus. 51. Unsurfaced, very old rammed-earth building in France.

Illus. 52. Very old rammed-earth home built in France on two levels.

Illus. 53. Another old, commercial rammed-earth building in France.

5

Firewood for Burning and Building

Each of these chapters begins with a brief history of its particular building concept. This provides one with a link to the present and stimulates a certain kinship with the builders of the past. Building in any medium is more than just techniques and plans, it is also an instinct. Every animal in nature has an instinct to create shelter for itself and its offspring. Man is no exception to this urge.

A good friend of mine, Jack Henstridge, of New Brunswick, Canada has done more building and consulting on cordwood houses than any other individual that I know. Jack is also quite a philosopher and includes his philosophy in his writings on cordwood. He has a very interesting thought on man's discovery and use of the cordwood wall for constructing a dwelling. Jack believes that the most precious discovery early man made was fire and its use. Since the match wasn't invented until some time later, keeping a fire going was very necessary. Towards this end, man stacked short pieces of firewood around the fire. Man discovered that by getting between the stacked wood and the fire he could stay warm and be shielded from the wind. Jack feels that it was a natural next step to add long poles over the surrounding firewood wall and then large leaves to keep the fire from being rained out and to keep the wood dry. Plugging the even ends on the inside of the surrounding firewood wall with mud kept the wind from coming though the cracks and the jagged ends to the outside provided an impenetrable fortress against enemies. Thus, the first cordwood house came into being, and man didn't need the cave any more, or so Jack says. For all I know, Jack is right since evidence of cordwood masonry probably predates recorded history.

When planning your own cordwood structure, plan either a solid slab or substantial footings. Both will have to be reinforced with steel. If a slab is indicated, your plumbing and some wiring will probably be in the slab. To keep from having to break the slab up at a later date to repair these utilities, provide chases that will allow access to wires and pipes. These chases should be large enough so that additional pipe and wire can be inserted and connected. Provide chases under and through footings also.

A cordwood wall is not as heavy as rammed earth, but it is still heavy and will require substantial base to stand securely. Do not skimp on footings! Once site preparation is complete and the footings are set enough to support the wall, you are ready to become a firewood mason.

Determining the type of wood that is available, along with the quantity and quality will be your next step. The main advantage of a firewood wall as opposed to a log wall is that there is no need for long, straight trees and thus the supply is greater. It may be necessary to cut live trees to supply your needs. If this is the case, try to choose those that need thinning so that the stronger, better shaped trees that are left will have a better chance to grow. It is not necessary to have hardwood since any soft wood will work just as well and will cure out much faster. (*Note*: remove the bark from the pieces as soon as they are cut or it will be nearly impossible once they have dried. Dead trees that are standing and solid are also a good source since the blocks will not have to cure or dry before using in the wall.) Pile the green blocks in the shade to dry and the pieces will not crack as much as if left in the sun to dry. A variety of woods will add color and interest to the wall texture. Also use a variety of diameters, and even split pieces. You are the sculptor—have fun!

There are a couple of ways to cut the blocks for your wall. The most efficient and quick way is to borrow an old farm buzz saw. These large circular saws make short work of firewood cutting. Set up a gauge on the carriage to mark the lengths desired and have at it. *Caution*: There are a number of people who have missing hands, arms, etc. These saws can be extremely dangerous, so always have a helper to lessen the chance of an accident. A chain saw also may be used. More care is needed with a chain saw to insure the pieces are all cut the same length and at the same angle. Some texture to the wall is good but too much tends to spoil its appearance.

One of the most frequently asked questions is: How do I figure how much wood will be needed to complete my house? One cord of wood will give you a section of wall that is eight feet high by sixteen feet long. This is figuring without mortar so you may actually get more wall than this when mortared but use the dry figure when calculating wood requirements. Remember, a cord of wood measures four by four by eight.

The one-foot length for exterior wall is not necessary for the interior dividing walls. These walls will work fine at six inches. This length gives a substantial wall without taking up too much of the interior space. Not many conventional homes can boast one-foot-thick exterior walls with six-inch interior walls that are nearly soundproof.

A balance is struck between mortar and wood. A wall with too little mortar tends to look exactly like dry stacked firewood and leaves a lot to be desired in appearance. The use of various sizes of blocks with attendant mortar distribution adds greatly to the appearance of the wall and reduces the quantity of wood needed.

The twentieth century saw the advent of portland cement and its many ramifications. Many of the houses in which it was used are already falling into severe disrepair. Concrete has absolutely no flex to it, thus it tends to break and crack. The older cement becomes, the more dry and brittle.

Lime mortar used in houses that were built in the eighteenth century is still intact. Part of the reason for this is that lime mortar has a certain amount of flexibility that keeps it from cracking in the normal freeze-thaw cycles of temperate climates. Lime mortar also has the added quality of self-healing. If a crack does open up, the lime in the mortar leaches into the crack and calcifies. If the crack is too large for self-healing, stuff loose lime in it and lightly irrigate. Since most people are familiar only with concrete, it may be necessary to do some experimenting with a lime mortar mix until it has the qualities you need.

Lime mortar withstands the ravages of time, but it also takes a great deal of time to set up. Early masons just used lime, sand and a dash of soda that produced carbon dioxide. It took so long for this mortar to set up that a house became a rather long-term project. Today's union labor prices would prohibit the use of this mortar. Lime was created over billions of years. Shellfish died and piled up on the ocean bottom, and carbon dioxide in the air and water turned them into limestone. You can make your own lime by burning shells in a fire and grinding them into powder. A much simpler method is to go to your handy building supply dealer's and buy hydrated lime. A ready-made solution exists in masonry cement, premixed. The convenience of premixed mortar is offset by cost, however, so I would suggest mixing your own to save money. It does take quite a lot of mud to build a cordwood wall.

The Mix: Twenty quarts of sand, five quarts of lime, three quarts of portland cement. A small cement mixer is necessary; otherwise it will be difficult to maintain any consistency doing it by hand in a mortar box. Jack Henstridge uses this mix in Canada. He indicates the farther south you live the less portland will be needed; i.e., six lime to two cement or seven lime to one cement. Be sure to keep eight of powder to twenty of sand to get a two and a half to one mix. Jack has a good measuring method that I like. He uses a five-gallon can for the sand, a five-quart pail for the lime and a three-quart plastic pail (the small pail used used by painters) for the portland cement.

How to Mix: Put the three dry ingredients into the mixer and let it rotate for about five minutes to be sure each grain of sand is coated with powder. Add a small amount of water. The amount will vary according to the amount of moisture in the sand. Add a little at a time. The main thing is to be sure the mix is not too loose. The mortar should form a ball and maintain its shape when released. Try to maintain this consistency in all batches. Quality control at this point will give a more uniform wall that will be strong and have less shrink cracks in it.
Note: A pair of heavy rubber gloves are essential to preserve your hands from the chemical action. You will find that you use your hands to apply the "mud" more than a trowel.

You now have your wood blocks cut and stacked close to your wall site, wet mortar and are ready to start being a wood mason. As soon as you empty the mixer, fill it with sand and powder and let it turn while you lay up the blocks. This will keep you moving right along and greatly reduce down time between batches. A plumb level or spirit level (a long one) is the next most important tool needed. The level is to keep the wall vertical. I have included two of Jack's designs for plumb levels to be used on both vertical and horizontal surfaces.

Begin laying your blocks by laying two rows of mortar on your slab, footing or

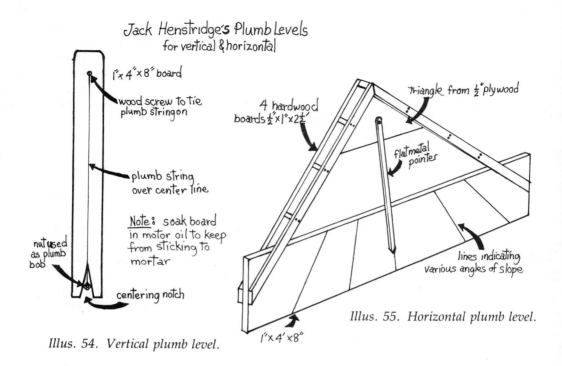

Jack Henstridge's Plumb Levels
for vertical & horizontal

1"x 4"x 8" board

wood screw to tie plumb string on

plumb string over center line

Note: soak board in motor oil to keep from sticking to mortar

nut used as plumb bob

centering notch

Illus. 54. Vertical plumb level.

4 hardwood boards ½"x1"x2½'

triangle from ½" plywood

flat metal pointer

lines indicating various angles of slope

1"x 4' x8"

Illus. 55. Horizontal plumb level.

foundation wall. Next place wood blocks on the mortar. Leave some space between the blocks in your first row or rank. Work around your building, not vertically. This is to allow the mortar to set up as the wall gains height. Use your hands and push mud into the spaces between the first row of blocks and place the next row. Never build higher around window and door frames just to see how the wall is going to look. If you do this, the next morning you will go out and find that the wall is leaning outward because the mortar could not support the vertical weight.

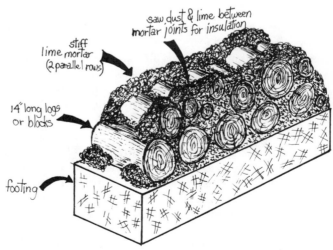

saw dust & lime between mortar joints for insulation

stiff lime mortar (2 parallel rows)

14" long logs or blocks

footing

Illus. 56. Cordwood/stackwood wall composition.

Once the first row of blocks is down, place two more rows of mud on them, filling down between them as well as on top. This will leave a void between the outside of the wall mortar and the inside. This void has to be filled with insulation to keep the mortar joints from conducting the warm inside air to the outside in the winter. You can pick up scrap plastic foam and such and break it into small pieces and place these pieces in the voids between the mortar joints. A readily available insulation has been created by your cutting the blocks for the walls: sawdust. Since sawdust is cellulose and one of the best insulators around, you don't have to scout around for a building materials dump. Mix two quarts of lime with five gallons of sawdust before pouring it dry into the voids between the blocks. The lime will prevent any insect infestation.

Illus. 57. Cordwood being laid. Note the dry mixture on mortar in two rows with lime/sawdust fill between for insulation.

When you think you have about ten minutes of mud left in your pail, add water to the dry mix in the mixer. This will keep you moving along without your having to wait for another batch. As the wall progresses, use your eye and mix wood sizes so the wall doesn't just become rows of blocks all the same size. As the wall goes up, rout some of the mortar out with your fingers from around the outside ends of the blocks. This gives the wall some texture and a very nice appearance.

Illus. 58. Here you see cordwood spacing and the variety of sizes as well as doubled-up three-by-fourteen-inch boards used for rafters on two-foot centers. Note the heavy window frame to withstand the soil pressure.

As the wall gains stature, keep checking it with your level to be sure that it is vertical. Tap it in or out before the mortar sets up or it is too late.

The top of the wall and the ceiling are your next big steps. You have no way to control the exact height of the wall due to the various sizes of blocks being used. Therefore you must build the ceiling joists or rafters ahead of time and place them on scaffolding to level them. The wall is then built up and around them. Do not build the wall above them, however; leave this until you board the roof in, then fill it in. Your cordwood wall has a lot going for it. It is soundproof, highly insulated, fireproof and the only heavy work is wheeling the mortar. The blocks are light and when completed, the wall is self-finished, both inside and outside.

Many people ask what they have to do to preserve the wood blocks. No preservative is needed. Let the blocks breathe. Also, don't try to lay the blocks in the winter or the mortar will freeze and crumble. If the weather is hot and dry, keep the wall moist by draping wet blankets over it until the next day; otherwise the mortar will dry and not cure. The result will be the same as from freezing, that is, the mortar will crumble. If you insist on changing the wall's appearance to look more conventional, whitewash it. Old fashioned whitewash will allow the wall to breathe while giving it a more conventional look. The main preservation of the wall will occur by not letting the wall come into contact with the ground. Insects only penetrate wood from the sides, not from the ends. The growth rings prevent the insects from invading the wood from the ends, so, you see, once again nature is looking out for you.

66

Illus. 59. Post-and-beam cordwood cottage.

If your house is round, all you need to make it uniform in circumference is a stake in the middle with a string attached with which you can swing an arc. A rectangular or square house has different problems. Jack feels that square corners are about as necessary as hemorrhoids, but you may have a more conventional view of design. Corners can be handled several ways. If you are using a post-and-beam framework, the corners are already taken care of and the cordwood is merely fill between the vertical posts and horizontal beams.

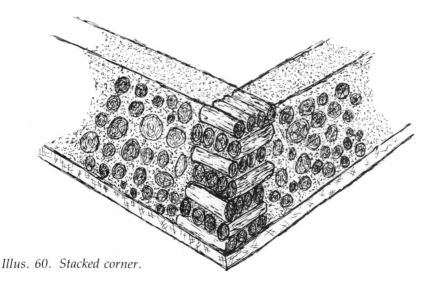

Illus. 60. Stacked corner.

The stacked corner is probably the simplest and strongest solution. Illus. 60 depicts the method for accomplishing this. It is the same method used for stacking firewood without it collapsing at the ends. Pieces are crosshatched and interlaced with the stack in order to tie it all together

Doors and windows present their own peculiar problems. Building the window frames is no particular problem since all you need to do is nail up a box out of two-by-twelves or whatever dimension will fit the thickness of wall. Since you are building the wall horizontally, just place the box on the wall at the height desired and build the wall around it. Secure the frame in place by driving four-inch nails through it into the blocks. Nails can be driven into the bottom of the frame prior to setting it on the wall to coincide with mortar joints. The combination will keep the frame securely in place as long as the structure stands.

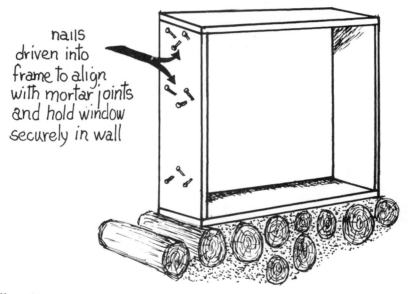

nails driven into frame to align with mortar joints and hold window securely in wall

Illus. 61.

Door frames present a problem when using two-inch thick lumber. A seven-foot two-by-twelve tends to warp or twist from the weight of a stout door. It is my suggestion that you use a couple of heavy timbers at the sides to prevent warping. Eight-inch thick timbers would be great.

Partition walls do not have to be cordwood unless you want the same appearance for all of the structure's walls. A standard two-by-four wall works well and is a snap to fasten to the outer walls since the two-by-fours can be easily nailed directly to the wall blocks. Rammed-earth walls work well and are nearly sound-proof.

The roof can be a post-and-beam affair or a rafter arrangement. I prefer a sod roof so a shallow pitch is necessary. As mentioned previously, a sod roof doesn't

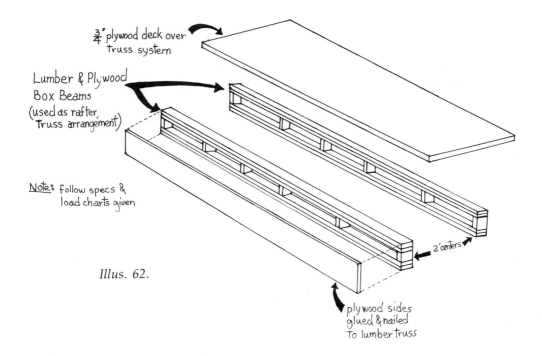

$\frac{3}{4}''$ plywood deck over truss system

Lumber & Plywood Box Beams (used as rafter, Truss arrangement)

Note: follow specs & load charts given

Illus. 62.

2' centers

plywood sides glued & nailed To lumber truss

have to have much thickness, just enough to sustain the grass. Five or six inches of good topsoil used as base for the sod is more than adequate. Choose your sod from a gravel pit area that has a low moisture base. The grass that has survived there will go wild with the good topsoil and thrive during times of drought. Illus. 62 depicts the construction of a truss support system for a sod roof. Remember, the sod roof will weigh considerably more than a conventional roof.

6

Mud and Adobe

This chapter will be of special interest to those who have long admired the grace, beauty and energy efficiency of the old traditional adobe homes of the southwest portion of the United States. The native Americans first used adobe in the construction of their hogans. As they came into contact with white settlers, their earth-building technology was mixed with more traditional eastern home designs to eventually evolve into the present-day designs.

Generally speaking, there are two classes of earth-wall construction—puddled and tamped. In the former, a molecular aggregation of earth particles is achieved with a liquid medium—a puddling process. In the second, the earth particles are compacted by the use of compression—a tamping process. Adobe blocks are puddled (wet); rammed earth is tamped (dry).

Whether puddled or tamped, the earth may be stabilized or unstabilized. The common stabilizer used in the puddling process is bitumen (mineral pitch or asphalt, or some of the semi-solid tars), while that employed in tamping is usually ordinary cement.

Finally, earth may be precast into blocks or cast into form in position. Walls of an owner-built home can, therefore, be pulled or tamped, stabilized or un-stabilized, precast or made in position.

One's choice of system depends upon a host of factors, such as design, building code, type of soil, facilities, equipment, and workers available near the building site.

It has been found that practically any soil can be somehow used in earth-wall construction. A soil which proves unsuitable for building by one method may be entirely satisfactory for another. For instance, a soil used in a poured adobe wall may shrink and crack, but the same soil may prove satisfactory for adobe blocks, since the blocks are "preshrunk" before being incorporated into the wall. Also in tamped earth methods, consolidation of earth particles reduces shrinkage.

The sandy clay adobe soil (with at least thirty percent sand and not less than fifty percent clay and silt) of the arid southwest United States is usually considered ideal for puddled earth wall construction. It is the clay that provides compression strength and the sand that reduces shrinkage and cracking, by lowering the moisture absorption. Adobe blocks are moulded from clay in a "plastic" state, often with a moisture content as high as thirty percent (fifteen to eighteen percent moisture content is considered optimum. Straw binder is sometimes used to reduce cracking in unstabilized blocks, the straw being cut in lengths from four to eight inches and evenly distributed throughout the mass. About one hundred fifty pounds of straw should be used to make one thousand blocks four by twelve by eighteen. Very little fibre decomposition will occur in the adobe block. Adobe blocks in the southwest over one hundred years old have been found to contain dried grasses in such perfect condition that the species could be identified.

The usual practice in America is to stabilize, or "waterproof" adobe blocks with an asphalt emulsion. Bitumul is an excellent commercial product produced by a Standard Oil Co. subsidary but is constantly on the petroleum-cost spiral. It would be less expensive to make an unstabilized block and waterproof it on the outside. Tests run by the U.S. Bureau of Standards show that stabilizing blocks does not appreciably increase their strength and the insulation value is reduced, since the density of the block is increased by the stabilizing process.

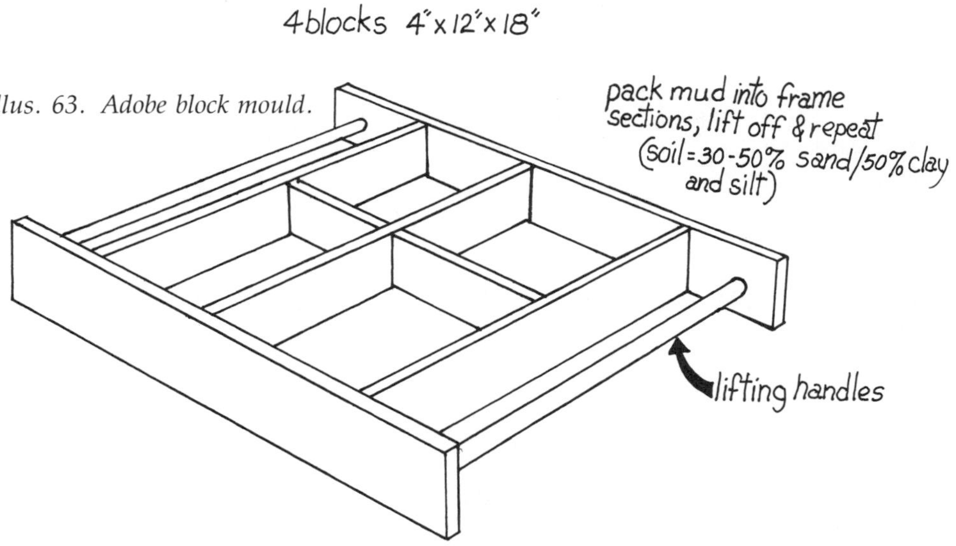

4 blocks 4" x 12" x 18"

Illus. 63. Adobe block mould.

pack mud into frame sections, lift off & repeat (soil = 30-50% sand/50% clay and silt)

lifting handles

A set of wooden forms for creating adobe blocks have been created by the Australian Commonwealth Experimental Building Station. These forms are as good as can be found anywhere. After the adobe mud is hand-moulded into the form, the form can be picked up and placed next to the removed blocks for the next casting. The fresh blocks should be kept in their original position for at least two to three days before moving to a drying shelter. Drying should be accomplished by standing the blocks on edge, leaving an air space between each row for more even curing. Cure the blocks for about three weeks before using. Blocks with a high clay content will require more time to cure out.

Mixing adobe by hand is slow and tedious. A mechanical mixer will greatly speed up the process of block-making and give a more even mix to the material. Generally speaking, a cement mixer will not work very well unless it is modified with blades or baffles to break up the material as the drum turns. The pug, dough or plaster mixer is ideal for mixing adobe and can be rented.

Bitumen stabilization is commonly used nowadays to waterproof the blocks. As stated previously, it can be costly and is not necessary. If you do choose to use this process, this type of asphalt emulsion mixes freely with soil of moderate to high clay content, as well as with water. While mixing, the water carries the bitumen into close contact with the clay particles, and as the water evaporates it is replaced by the bitumen. Soils with a high sand content (over fifty percent sand) should receive four to six percent emulsion by weight, while fine clay (less than fifty percent sand) requires thirteen to twenty percent emulsion. Sandy soil will require only ten percent liquid to bring the material to a workable state of plasticity whereas fine clay soil requires up to twenty percent.

The same material mix used for moulding the blocks can also be used for the mortar to lay the blocks. The use of the same material for both blocks and mortar will give both the same expansion coefficient. A small amount of cement can be added to the mortar to make it set faster and it will also strengthen the joints.

A simple test to determine the clay to sand content of your proposed block-making soil can be accomplished by filling a one-quart mason jar full of the soil sample (the earth should first be screened through a No. 4 sieve that is six squares per inch). Fill the jar with water and a spoonful of ordinary table salt to speed up the settling of the clay. Agitate the jar thoroughly and allow it to settle for one hour. The sand will settle to the bottom with the clay on top. Measure the height of the sand and divide it by that of the total of soil settled in the bottom of the jar; this will give the percentage of sand.

Illus. 64. Adobe roof layout. (Porch overhangs protect mud-block walls.)

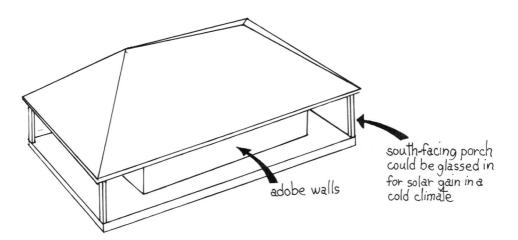

adobe walls

south-facing porch could be glassed in for solar gain in a cold climate

Contrary to what you may have heard, adobe can be used in almost any geographic area and climate. Damage usually occurs through dampness at or just above the ground level of an earth wall. This is particularly so in countries where it may freeze. The wall may be protected in a variety of ways. Stabilization is one option, although I feel there are better methods. A lime mortar plaster will endure well and protect the adobe blocks from both rain and snow. A raised foundation combined with a good roof overhang, porches and greenhouses also greatly increase the longevity of adobe or any earth wall. A design that takes advantage of the climate and cooperates with nature is always superior to applied wall coverings in protecting any structure. In most cases, a wall covering will not be necessary either.

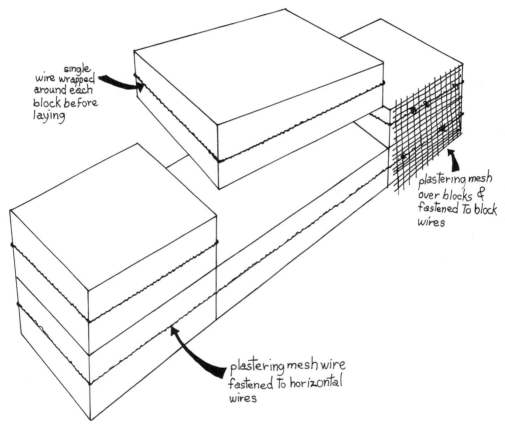

single wire wrapped around each block before laying

plastering mesh over blocks & fastened To block wires

plastering mesh wire fastened To horizontal wires

Illus. 65. Adobe block, wire mesh fastening system for surface plastering.

If a protective finish is applied to the outside of the adobe blocks, there are several precautions that should be taken. The most common mistake made in applying protective finishes to earth walls is to put the coating on before the wall is thoroughly dry. After the wall is completely dry, make sure the finish bonds with the wall or the wall will become wet due to condensation on the backside of the finish coat at the point where there is no bond. If the wall becomes saturated at that point, there is apt to be wall failure. A mesh wire such as chicken wire is usually used in this country and Mexico to help bond the coating of stucco to the

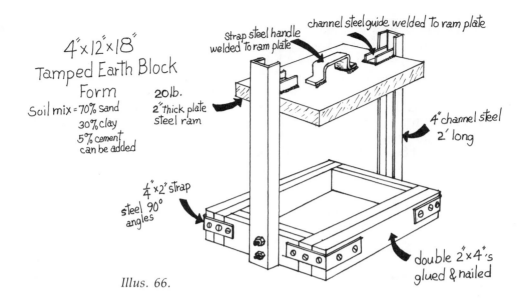

4″x 12″x 18″
Tamped Earth Block
Form

Soil mix = 70% sand
30% clay
5% cement
can be added

20 lb.
2″ thick plate
steel ram

strap steel handle
welded to ram plate

channel steel guide welded to ram plate

4″ channel steel
2′ long

¼″ x 2″ strap
steel 90°
angles

double 2″x 4″'s
glued & nailed

Illus. 66.

adobe blocks. The most common method of affixing the mesh to the blocks is to wrap a fixing wire around the block horizontally as it is being laid. Mesh can then be fastened to both the inside for plastering and the outside for applying stucco.

The Africans have had superior results in bonding a finish to their blocks without the use of mesh wire. The main reason for this evident success is the weak mix of cement to sand in their coating mix. Apparently the coating of a strong material (cement and lime) over a weaker material (earth) that is used predominantly in this country is an error. Differences in expansion and contraction cause a breaking in the bond between finish and wall. The African mix is one of cement and twelve of sand whereas we are accustomed to using a one to three mix and ten pounds of hydrated lime to each bag of cement.

At this point let me say that tamped-earth adobe blocks work just as well as puddled ones and take less time to cure before using in a wall. The forms have to be built more rigidly to withstand the expansion of the soil as it is compacted. It is easy to "blow" a form if it is not built out of stout enough material and bolted solid. The soil mix for tamped or rammed blocks is the same as for a formed rammed-earth wall. A mix of seventy percent sand and thirty percent clay is ideal. The mix should contain just enough moisture to form a ball in the hand when the mix is squeezed. When dropped on a hard surface, the ball should shatter, not splat. The addition of cement is not necessary, but one shovel of cement to twenty shovels of soil mix will add strength without greatly reducing insulative value.

Blocks can be made in a variety of sizes, but remember, dirt is heavy. Laying blocks can be accomplished with less strain if they are smaller. Since an adobe wall should be at least twelve inches thick to support the weight that will be imposed on it as well as act as a thermal retarder, the blocks should be at least twelve inches in one direction. A twelve-by-eighteen-inch block would work well and still be manageable. A four-inch thickness allows the blocks to dry more rapidly than a thicker one.

74

As in any structure where the weight of the wall is substantial, an adequate footing is essential. A footing similar to one used in a rammed-earth wall would work well. It is always good to have a compression test performed on the soil that is to bear the weight of your structure. A qualified engineer is also a good investment in order to have your footings figured adequately. Remember also that in areas that freeze, frost protection of the footings will have to be included to prevent frost heave that would break up the footing and wall. The ground will heave one quarter inch for each foot of soil depth that freezes. In some areas, the footings have to extend five feet down. It is also a good idea to protect them on the outside with rigid insulation. The footing width at the bottom has to be adequate to support the massive structure above without sinking to China or some other location. It is also good to plan the footings so they are at least six inches above grade so as to protect the lower wall from running water or standing water in event of heavy rain or snow melt. A one foot height above grade would be even better.

Illus. 67. Floor plan for adobe or tamped-earth block home (either underground or surface).

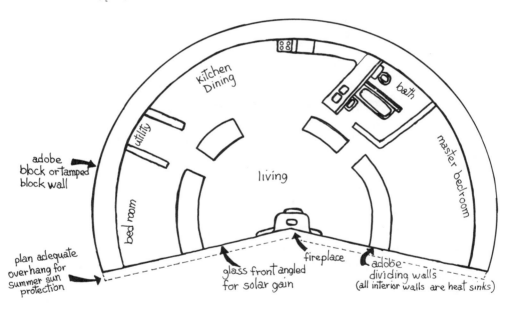

Door frames and window frames will have to be stout to handle the weight of the blocks that they will support over their tops. Doubled two-by-twelves would serve this purpose, but timbers that are custom cut four inches by twelve inches would be better.

Floors are optional but the previously mentioned treatments are all very workable. The main thing to remember about floor surfaces is the fact that you may be standing on them for various lengths of time and walking many miles on them in the course of your life, so they should be resilient and easy to care for. Any hard surface should be cushioned underneath. Everything from street or paving bricks to broken marble slabs can be laid into an interesting floor. I like to support these "hard" materials on a subfloor of concrete (or rammed earth) covered by one-half inch of rigid insulation covered by one-quarter inch of hardboard. "Soft" materials such as wood floors are ideal but usually expensive unless recycled materials can be located. Carpeting and various composition floor coverings are also nice but usually expensive.

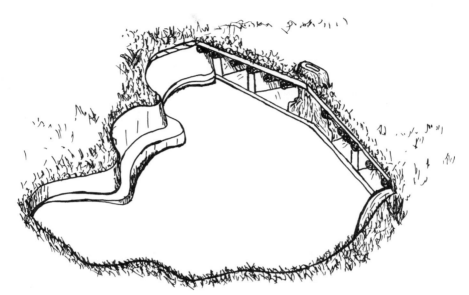

Illus. 68. Half-circle adobe or tamped-earth block home (underground).

The roof can also have various shapes and use a variety of weather stoppers, but again, I prefer a sod roof. A sod roof doesn't require a steep pitch and can be supported through the traditional pole rafters. Sod also doesn't erode when exposed to ultraviolet light and protects from hail and wind. Plan two-foot overhangs to protect the walls from water erosion.

The shape your home takes is up to you. I like curved walls and surfaces that blend with nature. Many of you will prefer square or rectangular designs and that is good, too, as long as they meet your personal needs. Follow the principles of good design outlined previously and adobe will serve you well.

In conclusion of this chapter I am going to include information on soil-cement blocks which can be used to build an adobe-style house also. Several years ago, a South African block maker invented an unusual machine for moulding soil-cement blocks. The Landcrete Machine is hand-operated and a sixty-pound pressure on a lever produces fifteen hundred pounds against the block. Two men operating the machine can produce enough blocks in two days to build an average-sized Asian home. That is nearly one thousand blocks per day. Each block is about five times the size of a red brick and twice as hard to crush. These blocks have the added feature of being made to interlock so that there is no need for mortar in laying them in a wall.

Structural tests have been made on identically proportioned hand- and

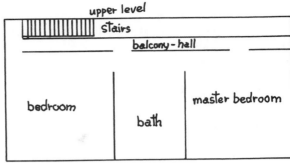

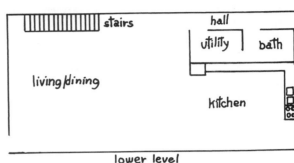

Illus. 69. Thirty-by-forty-foot
two-storey adobe.

upper level

stairs

balcony - hall

bedroom

bath

master bedroom

stairs

hall

utility

bath

living / dining

kitchen

lower level

machine-made compacted soil-cement blocks. Piers six feet high and eighteen inches square were constructed and loaded to failure. The hand-compacted blocks crushed at forty three pounds per square inch while Landcrete blocks crushed at one hundred twenty-one pounds per square inch. Machine-compacted blocks have been found to be structurally far superior to sun-dried blocks as well as hand-compacted soil cement varieties. They are so much stronger it is possible to reduce the outside bearing wall thickness to six inches instead of the usual twelve. In Colombia, six-inch earth blocks were used to construct buildings two stories in height. No more than five percent of cement needs to be added to a machine-compacted block.

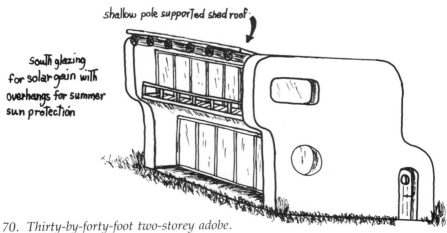

shallow pole supported shed roof

South glazing
for solar gain with
overhangs for summer
sun protection

Illus. 70. Thirty-by-forty-foot two-storey adobe.

The soil-cement block machine in use in Colombia (South America) was invented in 1957 at the Inter-American Housing and Planning Center, Bogotá. Paul Ramirez, a Chilean engineer and the inventor of the Cinva Ram, worked for several years developing a device which would give families of small means a manual tool to help them build durable walls and floors for their houses.

The Cinva Ram is a portable, hand-operated press for making block and floor tile; it consists of a metal mould in which damp, stabilized earth is compressed by a piston moved by a hand-operated lever mechanism. As a result of the lever system, a seventy-pound manual pressure produces a compression force of forty thousand pounds, a ratio twenty times better than the Landcrete Machine. The blocks are extruded by reverse action of the lever. They are removed and damp-cured for one week.

7

Still Dealing in Dirt—
Sod Still Works

The Omaha Indians constructed permanent earth lodges along the Missouri River where trees and willow poles were abundant. The stout frames of these lodges were cottonwood timbers. The surrounding "sheeting" was made up of willow poles placed vertically next to each other, then covered with grass bundles or thatch. An earthen wall ten or twelve feet thick at the bottom was constructed and the roof was covered with a shallow layer of earth and a carpet of sod blocks. Eastern Nebraska was the main area these earth lodges appeared because of the abundance of timber, but they were also found in limited numbers throughout the midwest or high plains of the United States.

The soddy was unique to Nebraska. It is believed that Mormons were the first to build sod houses in Nebraska as protection against the first hard winter in which they camped along the Missouri River just north of what is now Omaha. Most likely they derived part of their building strategy from the Omaha Indian earth lodges. The Mormons driven from Nauvoo, Illinois in large numbers were forced to winter on the Missouri and prepared for the inevitable starvation, disease and death. They only had a few months to build shelter and gather food against the onslaught of the terrible prairie winter. The log and sod houses prevented freezing but disease and hunger took their toll. Six hundred died and were buried in Nebraska soil that first winter.

The following spring they set out along the north side of the Platte River and continued to build sod houses on their journey across the "Great Grass Desert." A few of the Mormons stayed in Nebraska and created stopping posts for others that came later. These settlements were visited by other immigrants on their journeys and "Prairie Marble" architecture spread into Kansas and the Dakotas. This indigenous architecture continued from the middle eighteen hundreds into the early nineteen hundreds. The last sod house to have been built in the Nebraska

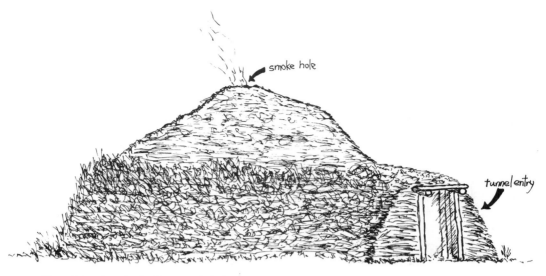

Illus. 71. Omaha Indian earth lodge. Frame is of cottonwood with creek willow filler; the outer cover is a six-inch-thick base of sod blocks with eight inches of dirt cover over the top.

sod house tradition was constructed by the Hersh family in 1940 near Dunning, Nebraska. The demise of this practical and beneficial architecture was not brought on because of a more worthy replacement, but rather by the desire to "conform."

The gold rush in California created a continual stream of fortune seekers back and forth across Nebraska. One of the early settlers in Lincoln counted fifty wagons going west and exactly fifty wagons going back east. Many of these disappointed fortune seekers settled in Nebraska on their way back east and found real prosperity in the land as ranchers, farmers and merchants. Forts sprang up with their accompanying communities. All of these early settlers had one thing in common—they were broke. Wagons returning from the west carried banners proclaiming, "In God we trusted, In Nebraska we busted."

Illus. 72. Rare two-storey sod home near Broken Bow, Nebraska, built around 1884 for $500.

Poverty and the lack of building materials forced the spread of sod construction throughout Nebraska, Kansas and the Dakotas. These dwellings were made without mortar, square, plumb or greenbacks. Contrary to most popular opinion, sod dwellings built toward the end of nineteenth century were very sophisticated in design concept. Some of the early dugouts and soddies were quite crude and

Illus. 73. Unusual home constructed from sod and hand-hewn cottonwood timber.

constructed only as temporary shelters. Later, even two-storey sod homes were created. These homes were cheap to build, were warm in winter, cool in summer and very comfortable. A statement recorded by one settler when writing to a relative stated; "The snow lay on the ground a long time, and the winter was cold. We had no coal but the house, built almost half underground with walls three feet thick and a dirt roof fifteen to eighteen inches thick, didn't need much fuel." In most cases the only fuels available were twisted prairie grass bundles and buffalo chips. Both of these fuels served well for cooking and heating the extremely efficient soddy. Tornadoes frequently tore away the roof—the soddy's weakest point—but even then the walls always remained standing and the families huddled inside were far safer than they would have been in frame houses, which can literally explode when hit by a tornado.

The sod house was a form of folk architecture and as a result also displayed the most common characteristic of folklore—variety. There was not one correct version of the soddy, only more or less common forms. Illus. 78—80 show the most common forms these dwellings took.

The essential ingredient is sod. Our modern suburban-industrial encroachment has all but destroyed any good native grasslands in or near large cities. There are, however, numerous rural areas in the midwest where brome, bluestem, buffalo grass and wire grass can still be found in significant quantities. If

Illus. 74. Unique sod-walled home with mud plaster held in place by branches taken from creek willows. The thatched roof of prairie grass was also unusual for the time.

Illus. 75. Although built in 1887, this modern-looking sod home shows the use of modern roofing material and well-framed windows.

Illus. 76. This soddy used sod for the roof, also. The overlapped pieces were worked as shingles. Note how they overhang the eaves to present a low wind-profile to the harsh Great Plains winds.

Illus. 77. Cottonwood timber homes with sod roofs.

you are fortunate enough to buy a good creek meadow, you will probably have a fairly good sod cover of native grass. The next ingredient for the proper sod house is the tool for cutting the sod from the prairie. The "cutting" or grasshopper plow was developed specifically for this job. A regular "turning" plow will not work since it digs deep and tumbles the sod, breaking and ruining it for building. The grasshopper plow had a flat shovel blade at the front that sheared the sod loose while long curved rods extending from the shovel to the side let it to the ground, gently and unbroken. If you ask around in the midwest, you can locate one still in usable condition. They are somewhat of a collector's item though many were made. Most likely one can be borrowed when the owner finds out you are actually going to use it to build a sod house.

Illus. 78. A simple rectangular soddy.

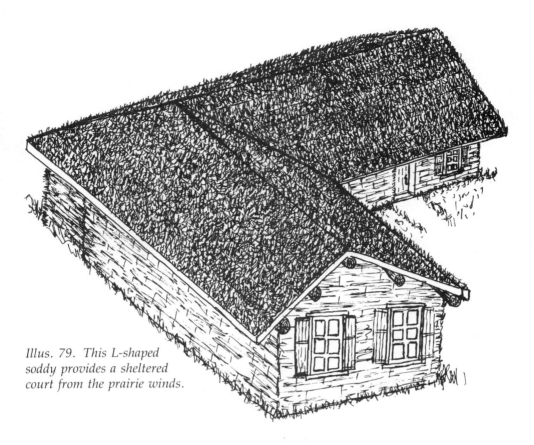

Illus. 79. This L-shaped soddy provides a sheltered court from the prairie winds.

Site preparation is next on the agenda. Most of the original soddies did not have footings or foundations and were generally built directly on the ground once the site was shaved clean of grass and levelled. I will describe and illustrate the methods used to create the sod houses of the American pioneers, then I will describe and illustrate some innovations that I think make sod a more viable modern building material. If the ground is packed hard enough, the heavy walls

Illus. 80. The T-shaped soddy provides windbreak for entry and extra room.

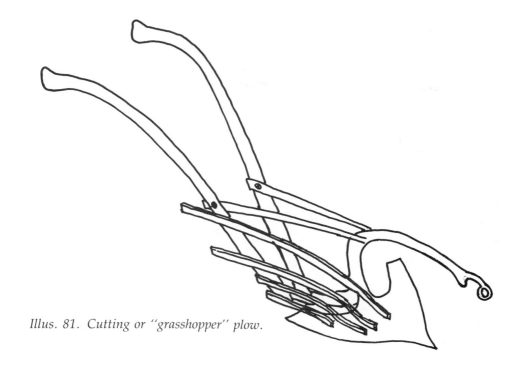

Illus. 81. Cutting or "grasshopper" plow.

can easily be supported without settling since their three-foot thickness distributes the weight over a fairly large area. Building an early design today, I would run a concrete footing to give added stability and to raise the sod off the ground and away from the runoff of rain from the eaves. If you do choose to build directly on the ground. you might want to bury some flat rocks at the corners where most of the structural weight is concentrated. Remember, the walls are three feet thick. At one-hundred-and-fifty pounds per cubic foot, soil is very heavy. A three-foot-by-three-foot section of wall will weigh in at four-thousand-fifty pounds. It is easy to see why these houses stood up to the winds of the prairie—any wind.

Illus. 82. Photo shows the cutting and hauling of sod blocks, sometimes called "prairie granite."

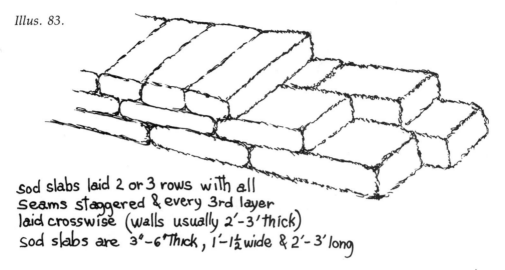

sod slabs laid 2 or 3 rows with all
seams staggered & every 3rd layer
laid crosswise (walls usually 2'-3' thick)
sod slabs are 3"-6" thick, 1'-1½ wide & 2'-3' long

Cutting the sod properly is very important. The cutting plow has to be pulled slowly in order to maintain a straight even and continuous strip of sod. The sod should be cut to a size that can easily be handled by a few workers. A piece of sod about three to four inches thick, one to one and a half feet wide and three feet long is about the maximum size a few people can handle. A low wagon or trailer is handy since the pieces do not have to be lifted very high. A heavy disc that has its blades spaced three feet apart can be run horizontally across the sod plow's path so that the sod strip will be in three-foot long pieces when it is turned by the plow.

Moisture content of the sod pieces is important to maintain their integrity as each is handled and laid in the wall. Cut only enough sod for one day's work and use it up so that it doesn't dry and get crumbly. The sod should be laid up by placing the grass side down. Three rows of blocks are laid side by side for the first

Illus. 84. *Excellent example, showing tapered walls to prevent the roof from pushing the tops of the walls outward.*

layer. The sod-block joints should be staggered so as to eliminate wind and insect encroachment. Two layers should be laid on top of each other in the same direction, then the third layer should serve as a binding layer and be laid across those below. This sandwiching keeps the parallel rows from separating. Any joints that do not seal or any cracks and holes should be filled and pounded tight with loose soil.

Illus. 85.   6″–8″ is built in above window frames To compensate for settling. The space, filled with cotton or fibreglass insulation, compresses without crushing window frame

As the wall progresses, great care has to be taken to insure the center line of the wall is perfectly vertical. Due to the great weight and mass of the wall, any lean will cause the wall to settle unevenly and eventually collapse. Some of the walls of the pioneer soddies were sloped or tapered. The inward slope of the wall toward the top helped stabilize the wall vertically against the outward thrust of the rafters that supported the heavy sod roofs. Just as when working with cordwood, work around the structure with a complete layer of sod before going to the next. Here again, set the window and door frame at the height desired and build up around them. Drive dowels or pegs through holes in the window frames into the surrounding sod blocks to hold the window firmly in place.

Illus. 85 shows the pioneer method of taking the upper weight of the sod wall off the window frame and keeping the window from being pinched as the sod settled. A space of six or seven inches was left above each frame and filled with cloth or paper wadding to absorb the settling. Fibreglass bat insulation would serve the same purpose. All of the little techniques that gave the structures functional use and integrity were a result of trial and error, so you can be assured these all work or they would not have continued.

The roof of the early soddy was very important since it not only kept the weather off the occupants but also protected the walls. If the roof failed, the sod

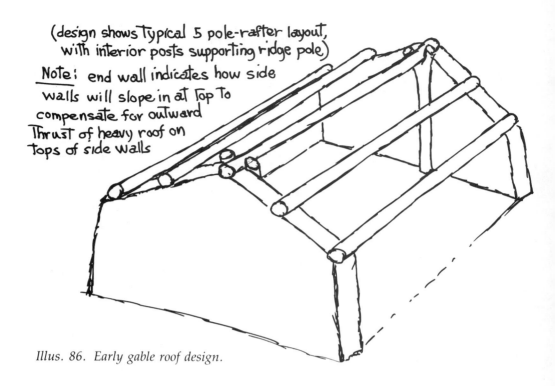

(design shows Typical 5 pole-rafter layout, with interior posts supporting ridge pole)

Note: end wall indicates how side walls will slope in at Top To compensate for outward Thrust of heavy roof on tops of side walls

Illus. 86. Early gable roof design.

house failed. The early settlers did not have the luxury of sawmills and lumber-yards to supply their needs so they used the few cedar poles they could find for beams and rafters. Instead of dimensional lumber for sheeting, they gathered willow poles and brush and used prairie grass for thatch beneath the sod pieces. These roofs weighed a lot and were not always structurally safe when saturated by prolonged rainy seasons. Many of these roofs collapsed on their occupants—often with tragic results. Several problems presented themselves when the early builders placed rafters and the weight of the roof directly upon the outer sod walls. The most immediate problem was one of settling, especially when the ridge pole was placed on the top of the end walls. As time progressed and the roof became saturated from rain, the side walls tended to slump outward and eventually collapse.

Several techniques were developed by these resourceful builders to cope with these problems. The best method of supporting the ridge pole was to place two vertical poles at the gable ends and place the ridge pole on them. This relieved the gable ends of most of the supporting task. Avoiding the thrust against the outside walls was not so simply solved. The best solution seemed to be that of thickening the base of the wall and slanting it inward at the top to provide counterthrust. Illus. 84 provides an excellent example of this.

Three roof types seem to have prevailed, although there were many adaptations. The gable roof, hipped and shed or lean-to were the most easily constructed and, therefore, the most popular. Illus. 86–88 depict the framing for these three types. The most common of the three types was the gable roof. These roofs ran from small (single-ridge pole with rafters to outside walls) to very large (ridge-pole and four beams). Numerous three-pole roofs were also constructed.

Illus. 87. Early hipped roof design.

Multiple layers helped insure that the roof would be strong and waterproof. As lumber became available the settlers used it for sheeting on their roofs and overlapped the boards in order to keep the roofs from leaking. Illus. 89 and 90 show the layers of material on the early structures, and then the more efficient system developed as lumber became available.

Due to the primitive conditions that the early settlers lived in, most people think of sod as something that is outdated and to be used only to construct a primitive dwelling. This is not so, combined with modern structural technology and some current materials, sod makes a most efficacious building material. The

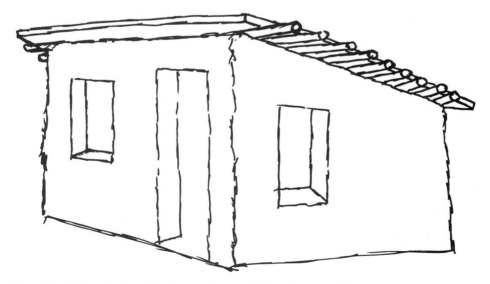

Illus. 88. Early shed roof design, using multiple poles as rafters.

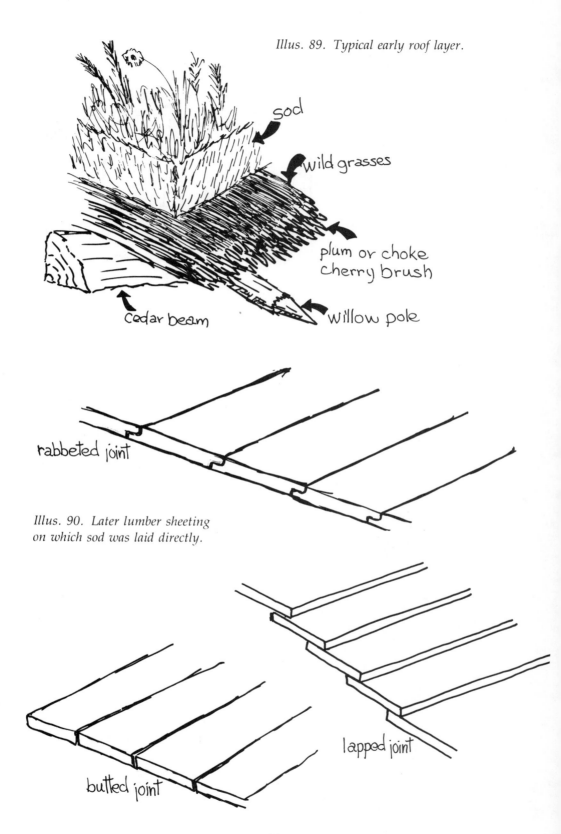

Illus. 89. Typical early roof layer.

sod

wild grasses

plum or choke
cherry brush

cedar beam

willow pole

rabbeted joint

*Illus. 90. Later lumber sheeting
on which sod was laid directly.*

lapped joint

butted joint

90

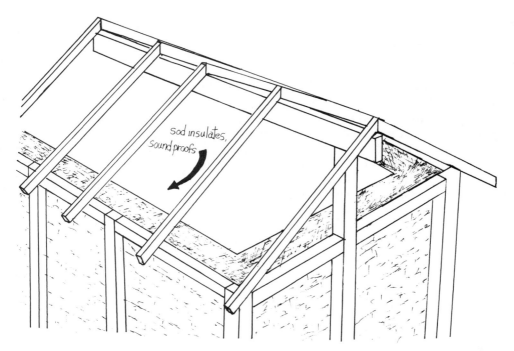

Illus. 91. Modern exterior post-and-beam frame with sod. The interior walls are on extended footing.

cutaway drawing (Illus. 91) shows how, when combined with a post-and-beam frame of either timber or concrete, the sod gives tremendous mass and thermal stability to a structure. The exterior can be plastered or left natural, depending on the effect desired. I still like a sod roof on a modern structure for the simple reason that it tempers the structure, helping to keep it cool in the summer and warm in the winter. Illus. 92 indicates roof structure and layers that could be incorporated with the post-and-beam frame.

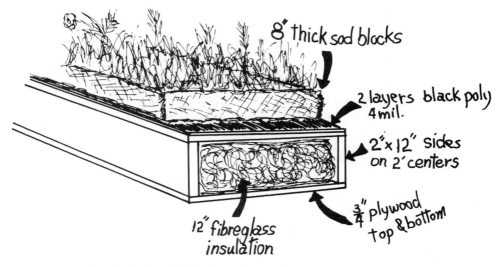

Illus. 92. Modern layered roof of sod.

Some handy hints or suggestions may be a good conclusion to this chapter. It is to be hoped that you are becoming convinced by this time that material does not dictate appearance and that even the most elementary of material, the earth, can be incorporated into modern design and esthetics. Due to the fact that the sod walls are three feet thick, natural light will not light much of an area except directly in front of the window. To remedy this situation, the inside of the window wells are shaved and angled to either side of the window frame. This angling of the walls around the windows allows the light to diffuse and light a much larger area. Another possibility, regarding the current use of sod as a building material: Experiment by constructing a small sod wall. Actually working with sod or any indigenous material is the best way to decide if it is a medium that suits your skills and energy. Many of my students are totally unenthusiastic about natural materials until they get their hands dirty. Most of us have been conditioned by conventional stick-and-nail technology. When you build a test wall of sod, cordwood, rammed earth or fieldstone and see how easily you have mastered the essential ingredients of building your own structural shell, your confidence and zeal will soar.

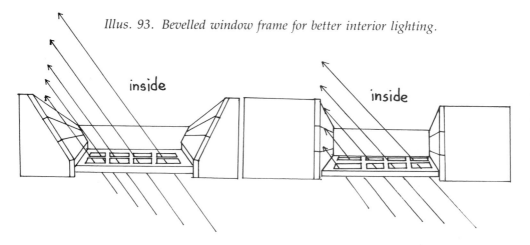

Illus. 93. Bevelled window frame for better interior lighting.

inside

inside

Sod and all indigenous material will meet some resistance from officialdom, so your own acquired knowledge through the building of a test wall will assure yourself and officialdom that this is still a viable means to an end. Combined with a post-and-beam frame, sod is not only simple to build with but is also very durable. To give your home a less primitive appearance, the exterior may be plastered over to hide the sod, stop any possible insect infestation and help protect it from weathering.

Roger L. Welsch wrote and researched a book titled *Sod Walls*.* Roger teaches at the University of Nebraska and is one of the most widely read and requested folklorists that I know. His research into the art of sod building was also an exciting journey into early Plains folklore. If you would like to gain additional insight and appreciation for this medium of building, go to your local library and check this book out.

*Roger L. Welsch, *Sod Walls*, Broken Bow, NE: Purcells, Inc., 1968.

8

Fitting Logs without Filling Cracks

Log cabins hold a fascination for many that cannot be displaced by any other form of construction or material. The first homes of the American Pilgrims were constructed of logs, along with successive dwellings as the population expanded westward. It wasn't until they ran out of trees in the Great Plains area that they had to change their building techniques.

Most of the cabins and log homes built by the settlers in their westward march were poorly constructed; depending in large part on slave cabin designs, originating in England. These designs were meant to be quick and easy to build, not necessarily weatherproof. The cabins usually had a rubble foundation for support and drainage, with the logs stacked on top of one another without fitting. The corners were either lap joints or dovetail joints to hold the logs in place. The gaps between the logs were chinked with mud or wattle and daub (a mix of mud, grass, twigs and available filler). The problem with this method of log-building is that the chinking shrinks and falls out and lets the wind blow through. Also the chinking is poor insulation. These buildings were meant to house slaves mainly and very little attention to detail or comfort was given. Many Americans don't know that there is any other method of log-building.

Fine homes, utilizing fitted logs with no space between the joints, were constructed by the Vikings and other Nordic tribes with access to good timber. The French also were tremendous craftsmen and built elaborate timber homes that incorporated many artistic features. During the eighteenth century, French military engineers and draftsmen were among the most skilled of professional classes. Plans they produced routinely were carefully drawn and tinted and are characterized by their meticulous detail as well as artistic embellishment. During this same period, ships' carpenters in Port Royal, Nova Scotia built fine log homes also and used their joinery talents to create some of the most beautiful truss-support systems for roofs that exist anywhere.

When considering the use of logs in your building plans, several things need to be taken into consideration. First, is the timber you wish to use available on your building site? If not, it may be impractical to further consider this medium, unless the hauling distance is very short. Secondly, are the trees under consideration long and straight enough? Last of all, as a log builder you have an obligation towards the conservation of trees and good log-building practices. This may seem academic, but it is also true.

Illus. 94. Slave log-cabin-building technique.

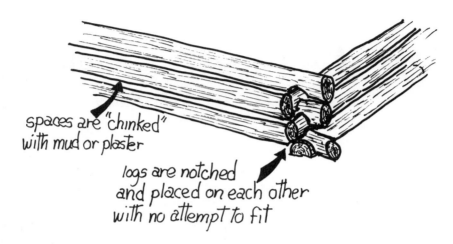

spaces are "chinked" with mud or plaster

logs are notched and placed on each other with no attempt to fit

B. Allan Mackie, a famous Canadian log builder and teacher of this trade states, "The pioneers of bygone centuries wasted timber on some small, bad buildings. They worked to survive, the trees were being felled and burned to create fields, and besides, they knew no better. We do . . . and so logs, in this day and age, ought to be the unthinkable materials for cabin-making. Let there be an end to the travesty of mimicking the worst that pioneers did while ignoring their best. The log builder is enjoying what could be the dying hours of a privileged profession, if care is not taken. If society is to allow him—and perhaps even to encourage him—to continue working in a medium so fast disappearing from even our most favoured regions, the log builder must lead the way in woods conservation. Let us resolve therefore to take sufficient time to log selectively . . . wherever possible . . . to work carefully . . . and produce log buildings of the highest order of beauty and excellence. It can be no other way, if we hope to continue building with logs."

When surveying the timber for your home design, ask yourself: *Does my design require the cutting of too much timber from the stand under consideration? Am I able to selectively cut trees so as to only thin and perhaps enhance the growing possibilities of the trees left? Will I be able to remove these trees from the place where they are standing without damaging other trees and animal habitat? Is my design worthy of the magnificent trees I intend to cut down?* If you can meet these criteria, then you are ready to be a log builder and will require the following technical information.

In order to build your log home properly, this list of tools is included for your benefit:

Chainsaw	Auger
Double-bitted axe	Basic set of carpenter's tools
Broadaxe	Dividers with level attached
Crosscut saw or framesaw	Scribers
Peeling spud	Log dogs

A pair of good scribers is vital since these are the key to measuring for perfectly fitted logs. Many different designs of scribers have been made by those who use them, but Illus. 95–99 will help you make a pair that will make your work easier. The scribers' job is to faithfully transfer the pattern of the log below to the surface of the log above. Scribers may also be used for finishing work along floors, partitions, windows and doors. The scriber points are set to the widest space showing between two logs. The cutting points are kept vertical, that is, directly above one another and the handle is held in as perfect a horizontal position as you can manage. A level mounted directly on the scriber will make the job of holding it in a horizontal position easier.

Illus. 95. Log scribers.

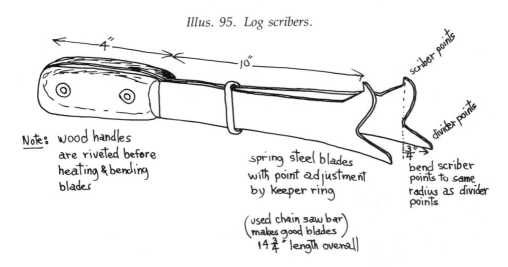

Note: wood handles are riveted before heating & bending blades

spring steel blades with point adjustment by keeper ring

(used chain saw bar makes good blades) 14¾" length overall

scriber points

divider points

3¾"

bend scriber points to same radius as divider points

The scribed line is continued over the notch if it is a round notch and on to the end of the log. Scribe both the inside and outside of the log. The whole idea of scribing is that the two lines formed are a constant vertical distance apart at any two points, one above the other. By cutting away the intervening wood on the top log, it will then drop to a perfect fit on the bottom log.

After the scribing of the top log is completed, roll it inward on the structure so the notching scores are upward. If the notch is to be cut with a chain saw, score along the scribe line with a chisel to prevent wood fraying. Work only on the side of the log near you so that you can see the line that you are working to. The lateral groove between the end notches should be a "V" cut to the inside edges of the scribed lines. The end or extended portion of the log outside of the notch should be coved out and not "Veed," then coved.

We will work through the entire building process next, so that each step is taken in the sequence of the actual construction. This will enable you to start your planning at a point to best consider the total concept.

Illus. 96. Log scribing.

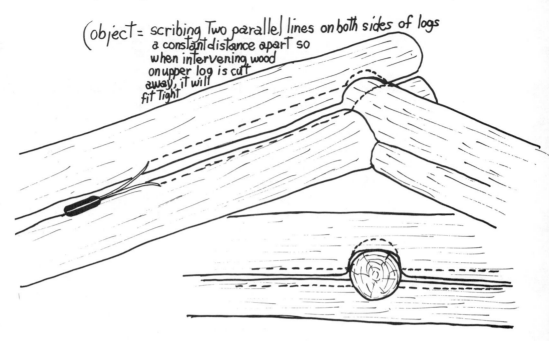

(object = scribing Two parallel lines on both sides of logs
a constant distance apart so
when intervening wood
on upper log is cut
away, it will
fit Tight

Illus. 97. Notch scribing.

(use divider points of
scriber for marking
notch)

depth of notch is equal to distance between logs

Illus. 98.

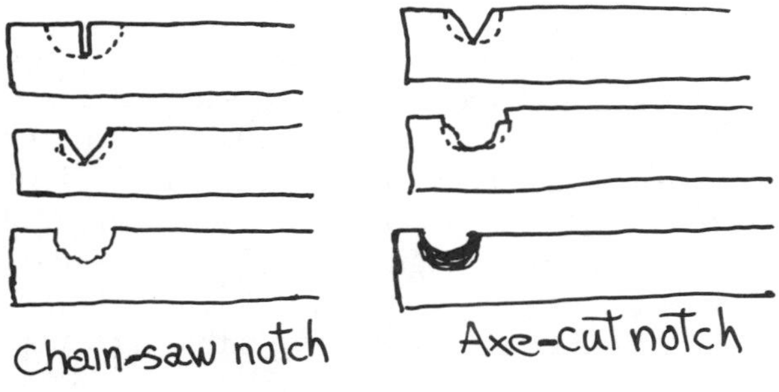

Chain-saw notch   Axe-cut notch

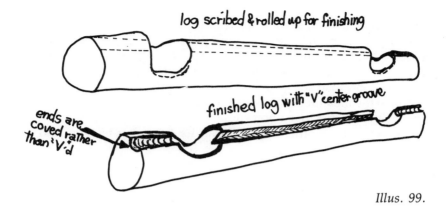

log scribed & rolled up for finishing

finished log with "V" center groove

ends are coved rather than "V'd"

Illus. 99.

BUILDING SITE

It is probably only in my mind, but to me it seems somewhat incongruous to take a spacious home that has been designed to blend into the forest and place it on a dinky lot in a congested suburb. If the lot were an acre, and the suburb was in a densely wooded area, I might consider it. The problem of transporting tremendously heavy material to the building site would still be a problem. If you are fortunate enough to live in a remote, scenic, wooded area, you have it on a downhill run for economic construction. Nevertheless, if your desire is to live in a city and you can arrange for the building material, then the site qualifications are no different than for any other home to be constructed on a foundation.

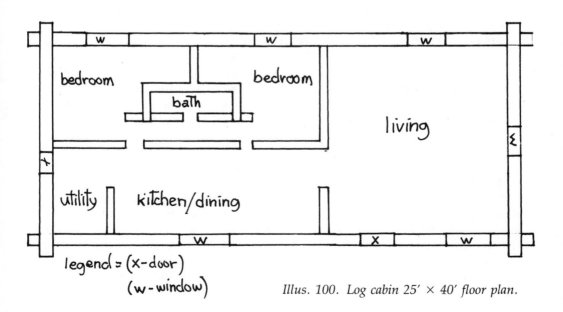

legend = (x-door)
(w-window)

Illus. 100. Log cabin 25' × 40' floor plan.

DESIGN

Here again, it is best to apply all of the principles of openness, passive solar orientation, low wind profile, etc. The floor plan shown in Illus. 100 would work very well for a log home. Just remember who is going to live in the home and design the space to fit the personalities involved. The mortgage companies and lending institutions instruct us to build for so-called resale value, a terrible contradiction to the meaning of a home, but a big stick they hold over the heads of the public. It seems to me that a home built for the total enjoyment of one family would be attractive to another one. So plan for your real feelings and human needs.

WHERE TO GET LOGS

There are three ways to get logs. One is to have them on the land that you own. Another is to cut them off of U.S. Forest Service land by getting a cutting permit. Another way is to get them from a commercial log producer. Logging companies will fill your order at varying prices, depending mostly on whether they are a large outfit that will charge an arm and a leg, or perhaps a gypo (man who cuts standing dead trees out of government timber). These small operators cut custom orders for lumber that they usually saw themselves for customers who want to build a boat dock, a deck or porch, etc. Shop around if you are in timber country; the prices can really vary.

SELECTING LOGS

When cruising timber to select your trees for cutting you will need to know the general diameters and lengths needed to construct your structure. As a rule, small buildings need smaller logs; large buildings need larger ones. If in doubt, always lean to the larger size rather than the smaller, since logs tend to shrink and the larger logs provide better insulation and give added strength to the home.

If your planned building is to be about thirty feet square, the logs will be about fourteen to sixteen inches at the butt. So while selecting trees, mark those that measure between forty-two and forty-eight inches in girth. To judge whether a tree is straight or not, stand back about one hundred feet and look at it from two sides at right angles to each other. If no crook or bend can be seen in the required length, stand close to the tree and sight up it. It must be very straight to appear so from this angle. There are not many perfectly straight trees, but if you are an amateur axeman, find the straightest trees possible.

Just about any of the varieties of trees that grow to log size can be used to build with, but some are more desirable than others. *Western Red Cedar* is excellent, but scarce and, therefore, expensive if you have to buy it. *Douglas Fir* is strong and many have a sweep that is distinctive. They make excellent rafters, joists, ridgepoles and logs. *Lodgepole Pine* have good form and strength and are easy to cut and peel. *Western Hemlock* is fairly soft but easy to work with and quite serviceable if kept protected. *Balsam* and other softwoods are easy to work with, straight and attractive, but will rot and decay easily so I would not use it. There are buildings one hundred years old still standing that are hewn out of *Poplar*, so I

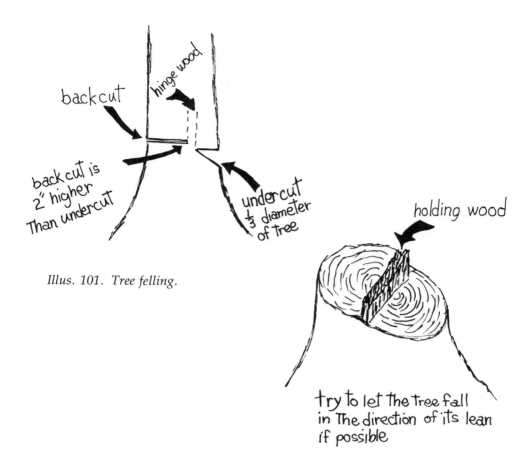

back cut

hinge wood

back cut is 2″ higher Than undercut

undercut ⅓ diameter of tree

holding wood

Illus. 101. Tree felling.

try to let the tree fall in The direction of its lean if possible

would not discount this fast-growing tree. This tree is being grown in four-acre plots for use as firewood. If one acre of trees is cut each year after four years of growth, these trees grow fast enough to supply a continual growth of firewood on only four acres. They tend to be straight as logs and are easy to work with. Poplar may eventually be one of the few trees that will be available to cut in the United States.

Hand-hewn logs of random proportions expertly assembled into a good building design, seem to bespeak the character of the builder and lend a certain aura to the home that is missing in the mass-produced, machine-peeled logs that are being shipped everywhere today as a sort of adult "Lincoln Log" design.

There is a difference between a wood chopper and a tree feller. The first just cuts through the tree and prays it doesn't fall on him or shatter when it hits or tears limbs off the surrounding forest. The second expertly determines the direction of the lean or weight of the tree in respect to the stump, and cuts it to fall in that direction or wedges it to fall in the direction desired. The main thing is to cut the tree to fall where it can be skidded out without damaging it or other trees. Begin cutting by starting the undercut on the side towards the direction you expect it to fall. The undercut should be about one quarter the diameter of the tree. Cut straight into the tree with one cut, then make a wedge cut slightly lower that chips out an opening that will allow the tree to fall. Begin the undercut as close to the ground as possible. The backcut is begun parallel to the undercut about two inches higher on the opposite side of the tree. After the saw has cut the depth of the blade into the tree, wedge the cut to keep the saw from pinching. Cut to within one inch of the undercut. The tree should begin falling in the direction of the undercut. If it doesn't, drive the wedge in further to lift the tree in that direction. A really stubborn tree may require two wedges. If the tree begins to lean to one side of where you want it to fall, leave a little extra hinge wood on the offside to help direct the tree. Always plan a getaway path once the tree begins to fall. Grab your saw and head in a direction to one side of the fall. If you move in the opposite direction, the falling tree may kick its butt up and back, catching you en route. If the saw sticks, leave it! Never cut trees on windy days and always take a friend and wear a hardhat.

Cut your peeling logs in the winter when the sap is down. Also, logs can be skidded on snow with less mechanical damage. Late fall is the next best cutting time, with summer last. Don't cut in spring since these logs will be swollen with sap and susceptible to checking and will cure out much slower. For optimum curing, the Scandinavians topped their trees, leaving two branches at the top. They then peeled two strips of bark off the tree as the workmen returned to the ground. This more "natural death" of the tree after it was left standing this way for two years seemed to cure the wood without checking and otherwise preserved its beauty and integrity. This may seem like a long time, but if you are cutting green wood, you will still need to cure the logs for two years in a sheltered location. The trees left standing will not need storage or handling until you are ready to build with them, so why all the hurry to cut? This is another reason to use a gypo who cuts only dead (cured) trees. The fact that many of the Scandinavian log homes date back to the fourteenth century and show little sign of deterioration also speaks well for this method of curing. Don't peel the logs until you are ready to build. The bark protects against checking, cracking, weathering and mechanical damage.

PREPARATION OF BUILDING SITE

Great amounts of time, money and energy have gone into finding and procuring your building site; it is to be hoped that the planning of the actual construction area will receive no less attention. Check first of all to be sure there are no legal ramifications to the actual placement of your design on the site. If you choose an ideal solar orientation for your home, then discover that it cannot face that direction due to setbacks required by the city or township involved, the function of your design may suffer. Test the soil for mineral content. The type of soil determines its bearing capacity, drainage capabilities, and also its leaching properties on the materials that will come in contact with it during and after construction. The borings that are analyzed should be taken to a depth that will also determine the underlying bearing capacity. Next a standard, ball-drop test for compression loads should be performed by a qualified engineer. This relative small investment is the stuff your home will literally rest on. Check with a county agent or local well driller if your property is rural. These people will have an excellent idea as to the problems of your soil. About the only time these tests would be unnecessary would be if you are building on a rock base. If you are, and the entire building site

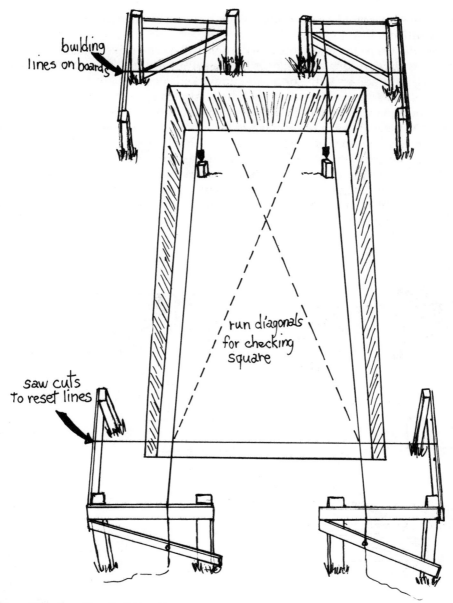

building
lines on boards

run diagonals
for checking
square

saw cuts
to reset lines

Illus. 102. Locating building lines.

is rock, then you may also have a problem locating and reaching water for your home. If all of these areas check out, then you are ready to string out your site for basement excavation or the preparation of footings.

Since this chapter deals with log construction, the prevalent shapes that lend themselves to ease of construction and best use of materials are the square and rectangle. Multiple-sided structures are possible, but more difficult. One of the reasons I like round buildings is that once a center stake is placed and an arc struck, everything within that arc will be true; not so the rectangle and square.

Staking out your building need not involve a surveyor unless property lines need to be verified.

Decide where any one of the four corners will be and drive a stake. Next, place a square with fairly long appendages in that corner and run string that aligns with the arms of the square to the opposite, unmarked corner, then check each corner with the square for accuracy. As a final check, stretch string from opposite corners across the square or rectangle. Next, where the strings cross in the center and form an X, measure each leg of the X to be sure that all four are the same length. You now have an accurate rectangle or square.

Since the actual excavation should be at least three feet larger than the actual building, corners for the excavation have to be marked in such a way that they will stand after the digging to allow the actual building's perimeter to be re-established. To accomplish this, extend the legs of the X. Erect ninety-degree corners out of stakes and boards at the appropriate digging distance. Next run

Illus. 103. Footings and foundations.

string from the arms of the digging corner boards to each corner of the digging locators, making sure each string is over the building's true perimeter lines. Saw notches on the boards where the strings are fastened so that when the excavation is complete, the strings may be put back on those notches and a plumb line dropped from the corners formed by the strings and thus the corners of the building re-established in the excavation. If no basement is to be dug, then the expanded digging site is not necessary and the actual building perimeter previously staked may be used to establish the footings.

FOOTINGS

Several footings and foundations are shown in Illus. 103 to give you options with regard to how you will build the floor of your home and support it. Each foundation has its purpose and benefits, just choose the one that will best suit your particular needs.

FLOORS AND JOISTS

Either log floor joists or two-by-tens may be used. If logs are used, all of the butts should be in the same direction. Thought as to span and spacing of the joists should be given careful considerations so that the flooring has proper support. As the footing illustrations indicate, the joists may be carried on the foundation, fastened into the bottom half of a wall log, or supported underneath by other logs or support material. There really is no correct or incorrect method, just what works best for your particular circumstances. If log joists are used, you may find it necessary to hew a portion of the log off to provide a flat surface that will secure the log. Insulation will also be required to keep the floors warm.

WALLS

The first logs placed on the foundation should be hewed in order to place them without rolling off the wall. (Note Illus. 106.) Once the first logs are placed, the wall may be continued, using the information with regard to notching, grooving and coving the upper logs that was given previously. Use your largest logs at the bottom of the wall. They will not only provide added strength, but are also the most difficult to handle. Remember to switch the butt ends of logs on each tier to balance the wall as it goes up.

Roll the logs up on the wall and to a place where they can be scribed in an optimum position. That position will be one that will allow the straightest wall with the least wood removed. Cut the notches so that the log will be lowered to within one or two inches of the log below. Roll the log on top of the lower log for scribing. Roll the log back on the side walls again and make the cuts. Insert the insulation filler and place the log on the bottom one and check the seal. If it fits properly, move on to the next log placement. Line up log ends on centers and place a sighting post at the end of each wall to sight the center line of log. This will keep your walls true. You may want to trim only every other log end, leaving the

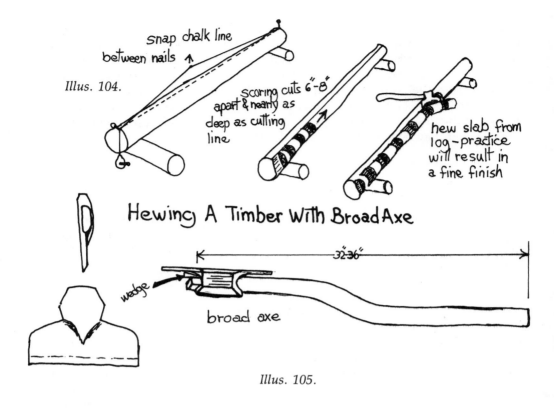

snap chalk line between nails ↑

Illus. 104.

scoring cuts 6"-8" apart & nearly as deep as cutting line

hew slab from log – practice will result in a fine finish

Hewing A Timber With Broad Axe

wedge

broad axe

32-36"

Illus. 105.

others to place scaffolding on. Insulation between logs can be several materials. Since the logs are very nearly airtight because of their proper fitting, only a small amount of insulation will be required to make the wall thermally tight. Fibreglass may be used as a filler in the groove, but sphagnum moss is superior if available.

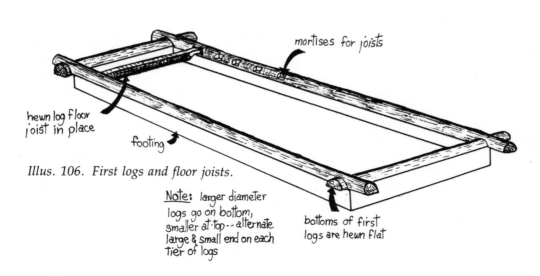

mortises for joists

hewn log floor joist in place

footing

Illus. 106. First logs and floor joists.

Note: larger diameter logs go on bottom, smaller at top -- alternate large & small end on each tier of logs

bottoms of first logs are hewn flat

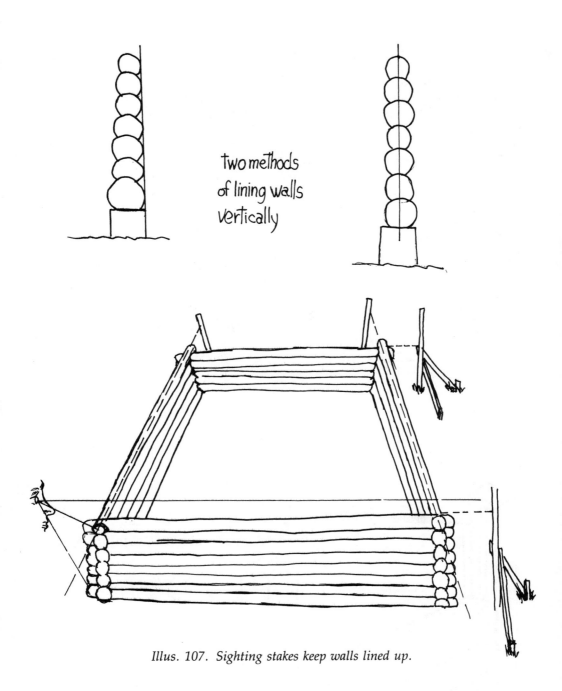

two methods
of lining walls
vertically

Illus. 107. Sighting stakes keep walls lined up.

Contrary to what many might think of moss, it is very sanitary and will not attract bugs. If stored it dries, so just sprinkle it before stuffing and it will become pliable. Once stuffed, the moss dries very quickly and conforms to the joint better than any other material. After three logs have been placed, drive wedges between the logs to raise them, stuff the moss in and knock the wedges out. The seal will be airtight.

This is sort of a backtrack, but may be beneficial at this point. After reading the beginning of this chapter, you may decide it will not be practical to build with logs since most of the logs available are too short. There is a method of building with short logs that works well. During the late nineteenth century the American army built fort structures out of short logs cut from scrub pine from the buttes near what is now Crawford, Nebraska. These buildings at Fort Robinson have since been re-created on the site in the same manner as originally built.

Illus. 108. Pièce-en-pièce construction.

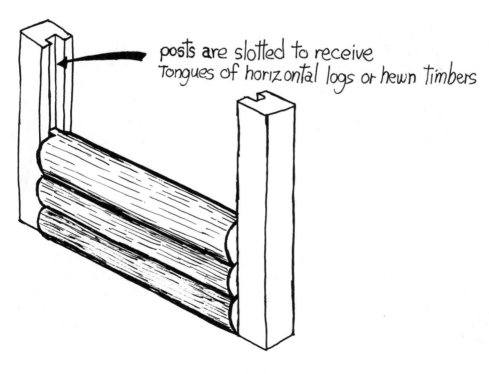

The method for building with short logs or hewn timber is called *Pièce-en-pièce* construction. It is a method where the timbers or logs are stacked on each other in short sections and held in place by vertical log or timber posts. Basically the structure is a post-and-beam frame made of log or hewn timbers and filled with logs or hewn timber pieces. The vertical posts are slotted to hold the tongues at each end of the horizontal logs or timbers. If short logs are used, they can be scribed, and grooved the same as in the use of long logs. Corners may be vertical posts or the various corners illustrated. Posts at the corners would take less of the log length than dovetail, lapped joints or coved joints.

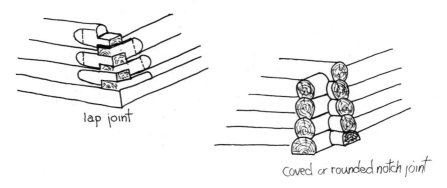

lap joint

Coved or rounded notch joint

Illus. 109. Joint corner and notch.

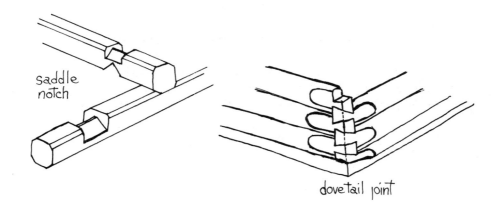

saddle notch

dovetail joint

PLACING LOGS ON BUILDING

Due to the size and weight of long logs, a means of raising them into position safely must be developed. I stress safely because if a log breaks loose it is apt to crush anyone and anything in its path. Illus. 110 shows the safest and most direct method of positioning logs on the structure. Skids and a rope pull work very well. Three men are needed, two with peaveys to guide the log up the skids and a third to operate the rope pull. The rope pull may use a manual winch or a powered one. Position the rope on the log being raised so that the small end of the log leads the large end up the skids since it will make less revolutions than the large end. A power crane or boom truck would be easier to use but is probably more costly and would require more space near the building to operate than the use of skids would.

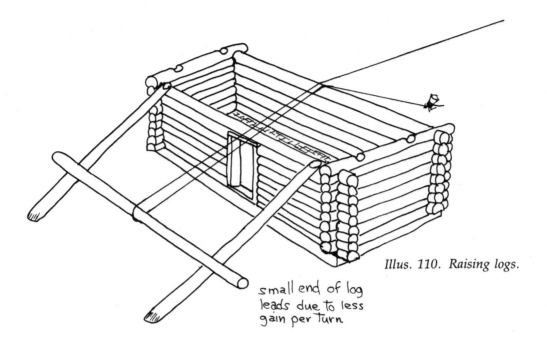

small end of log leads due to less gain per turn

Illus. 110. Raising logs.

FRAMING WINDOWS AND DOORS

A keyway is cut in the ends of the logs on either side of the window or door opening large enough to insert a two-by-four. This member holds the logs and acts as a nailing piece for the doorjamb and the sides of window frames. Be sure to

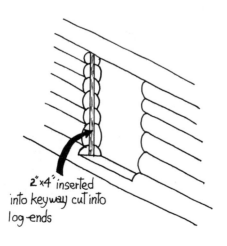

2"x4" inserted into keyway cut into log-ends

Illus. 111. Window and door openings.

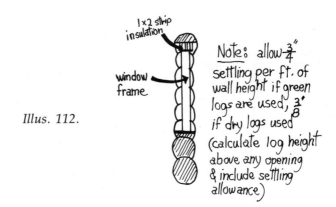

Illus. 112.

Note: allow $\frac{3}{4}''$ settling per ft. of wall height if green logs are used, $\frac{3}{8}'$ if dry logs used (calculate log height above any opening & include settling allowance)

leave space at the top of the door and windows that will allow settling. Walls constructed of green logs will settle about three-quarters of an inch per foot of wall height. Shrinking will not occur in width of window or door openings, but settling allowances must be made at all points where vertical forces exist. Even the use of dry logs will not appreciably reduce settling since it occurs due to the tightening of the log work. There will be less settling by using dry logs; approximately three-eighths of an inch per foot of wall. Prepare space in the header log for the settling and stuff the space with insulation.

GABLE ENDS, PURLINS AND RAFTERS

Now that you have created the walls, windows, doors, floors and room dividers, the roof has to be put on. There are several kinds of roofs that can be considered, but probably the one that will be the easiest to complete and give your structure a pleasing appearance is the gabled roof. When the top of the walls are completed,

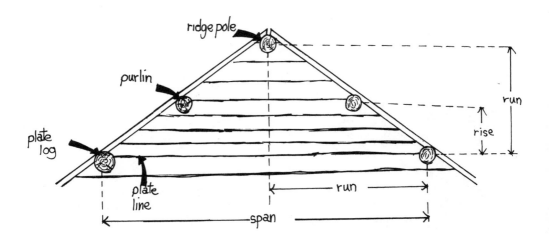

Illus. 113.

109

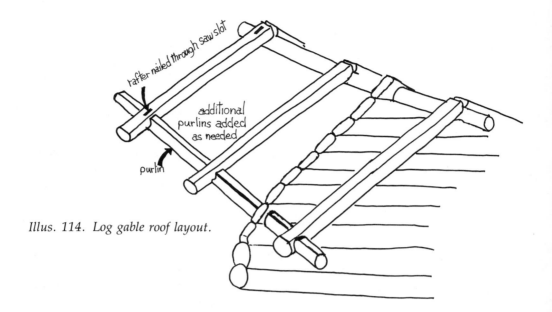

Illus. 114. Log gable roof layout.

the gable ends may be made using logs or framed with lumber or timbers. The gable end made of logs is held in place by purlins which are simply logs reaching the length of the building but lined up with the anticipated ridge. These logs will be lower than the roof line by about four inches to allow room for the rafters. Gable-end logs may be pinned in place by boring two two-inch auger holes through the log and the log below, then driving a two-inch square peg into the hole. Purlins should be double-notched into the log below.

If the building is too long for the purlins to hold the weight of the rafters, sheeting and roofing plus a snow load, then some interim support will have to be provided for them. The best means of providing that support is through the use of trusses. Illus. 115 shows an easy truss that is attractive and strong. These trusses

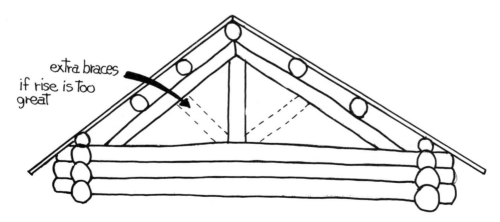

Illus. 115. Truss for interim support, when building is too long for just purlins.

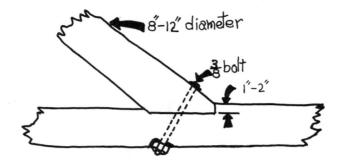

Illus. 116. Thrust joint.

should be placed every fifteen feet to give adequate support to the purlins. Although dimensional lumber may be used in a number of places in a log home, I prefer using logs and log pieces as much as possible to give the home a feeling of continuity, strength and natural beauty. All of the finishing touches that give a home personality will have to be provided by your imagination, good taste and sense of proportion, so have at it. I will complete this chapter with the thought that if you are an amateur log builder, you could certainly use some experienced help. In timber country you can usually find an experienced man in the local pub during the off-season who will be happy to give advice on his favorite subject; so here's a toast to your log home.

9

A Rolling Stone Gathers No Moss

I imagine that most of us have a stereotyped image of the first man to build a home. He is wearing animal skins, dragging a club in one hand and stacking rocks with the other. There is evidence, however, that due to the lack of knowledge regarding the means to bond the rocks together they were probably one of the last materials used to build a home. Stacking precisely cut quarry stones of immense size to build tombs and temples dates back thousands of years, but those structures required thousands of workers. All that was available to the average person in early history was rubble, stones broken naturally by nature and available at random locations. These small, often rounded stones could not readily be stacked into a wall without mortar to hold them in place.

The previous chapters have covered many materials, both natural and man-made. We have looked at aesthetics, building techniques and mechanics as well as the philosophy of building your own home. We will now discuss antiquity.

Stone was formed before any of the other properties of our earth. It comes in many varieties, each containing its own history of formation. I am not a geologist, but even a layperson can observe many things about a stone by merely examining it. Some stone is soft and crumbly, other stone is hard enough to defy cutting or breaking. Some stones have an almost woodlike grain to them, while others are sandy in texture. Some are smooth and rounded and others are rough or jagged. There are reddish hued stones that may contain iron, and greenish ones that may contain copper. As you contemplate building with stone, try to gain an appreciation for stones by studying them while hiking or camping.

After you have gained an appreciation for using stone as a possible building material, there are a few preliminary things that need to be explained before you start gathering rocks for your castle. If a quantity of stone is available on your land or near, and it is a quality that is suitable for building with, then you will have to decide how to use the stone to best advantage.

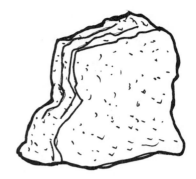

Illus. 117. Veneer stone.

There are three basic ways of using stone as a building material. A wall may be laid by fitting stones in a stack wall, using mortar as a filler. Facing a wall with stone for nonstructural purposes is another method of using stone. Formed masonry is the third method. A brief explanation of each method at this point may help you decide how best to use the stone available to you.

Illus. 118. Laying stone.

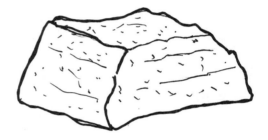

Because stone is very heavy, your footings and other site considerations will be the same as for the other heavy material designs discussed previously. Many of the modern homes use stone over another structural wall as a veneer for aesthetic purposes only. Since the subwall bears the weight of the building, the stones are usually thin slabs that are mortared in a thin decorative wall that is attached to the structural wall through the use of metal strips or clips. Facing stone is usually thin and flat.

A laid wall will use stones that are thicker with flattened surfaces that form rectangles, squares, triangles and other geometric shapes. The main thing to consider here is how the stones will stack in the wall, sitting solidly on one another without mortar. The mortar should only be a filler and sealer, not be used to overcome gravity in a laid wall.

Illus. 119. Forming stones.

Illus. 120.

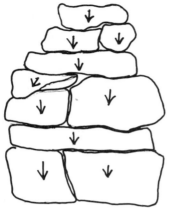

Good Pier
(most stones distribute
Their weight over Two
below and cross joints)

Poor Pier
(rocks push in all directions
and not all rest on at least
two below and cross joints)

Illus. 121.

Poorly Laid Wall

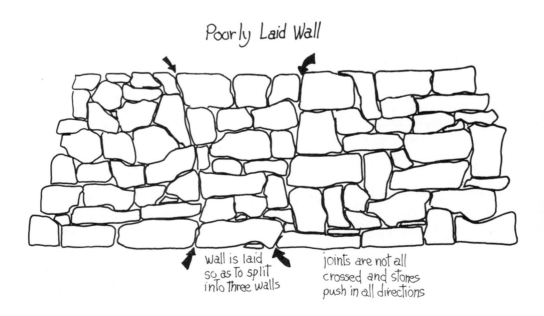

Wall is laid
so as To split
into Three walls

joints are not all
crossed and stones
push in all directions

Rounded stones of the kind found in some farm fields and in and around creeks or rivers lend themselves best to formed masonry. Formed masonry uses a variety of forms (generally movable) to hold the stone against the form sides while the center or back is poured with cement. The cement is expulsed between the stones, thus bonding them to the poured wall. There are several methods of accomplishing this type of masonry and we will discuss them in detail later in the chapter.

There are not too many types of stone that cannot be used to build with. If the stone is too soft or crumbly, or has too many fissures, it may not be desirable, but generally any stone may be used in one of the three forms mentioned.

Almost every layperson with little or no experience in building tends to look upon those who do as mystics. All I can say is that there is no magic to building, using the techniques in this book. There is a great amount of determination and sweat required and that is all. There is no way you can sit and read this book and gain the experience to build your home. This book will give you information which you need to assimilate then apply by actually getting your hands on the tools and materials. It is scary to begin a project of this size but once started, your confidence will build. *Start!*

Once understood, stone masonry is little more than carrying rocks and placing them on top of one another so that gravity will not make them fall. This may sound like an over-simplification but it is not. Deciding which form of stone masonry best fits the type of rock available to you is the first step.

LAID STONE

If your stone is the type that lends itself to laying, there are two basic principles involved. Gravity is the first principle that many novice and some experienced masons overlook. This may sound redundant, but it is vital to any laid wall. Gravity is implacable. Its constant force is evident in many poorly laid stone walls. Many of these walls were laid, using mortar as a glue to defy gravity. This technique will work temporarily, but eventually gravity wins and cracks develop. As you unload your rock at the building site, notice how the rocks settle naturally into a stable pile. The reason for this is that every stone has a center of gravity. Throw a stone and it will land on its most stable side. When laying stone, be sure to place them so they sit naturally and are totally stable without mortar.

The second principle of laying stone is to always lay a stone so that it will distribute its weight over at least two other stones below. All stones should be stable without the use of mortar and fit as tightly as possible. Good masonry then is not only the lifting and placing of stones, but also requires a lot of planning ahead. Illus. 120 and 121 indicate the fallacy of not following these two basic principles.

Everything should interlock along the entire wall. The mason who built the wall in Illus. 121, without realizing it, built it to separate at the points indicated by the arrows. Following these two principles takes careful planning as you proceed with a wall. Selecting stones that are not flawed and that fit together is a slow business requiring patience. You will see numerous examples of hasty and poorly planned masonry if you start looking. Good laying stone is important. If you run short or perhaps are looking for laying stone that is more suitable than what is

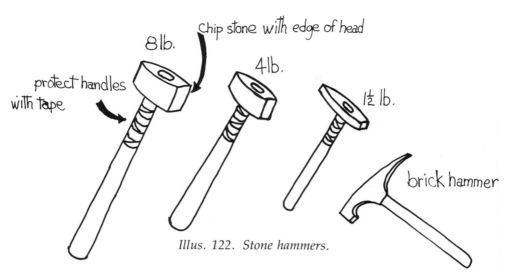

Illus. 122. Stone hammers.

available, you might consider going to a quarry. If you load and haul, the price of quarried stone is not that high. A lot of quarries do not cut building stone but rather cut stone for crushing and for rip-rap. Rip-rap is used for stabilizing river banks and other embankments. These stones weigh from twenty-five pounds to several hundred. Some of this stone makes good laying stone and is fairly cheap. Cut stone for laying may be too symmetric for some, so natural laying stones may also be found in stream beds and along roadsides. Fieldstone, if not too rounded, may also be used. Other than dirt, stone is the most plentiful building material, so go for well-proportioned stones and lay a wall that will stand as a memorial to your patience and craftsmanship long after your journey.

When selecting a stone to fill a space in the wall, it should be judged three ways. The top, base and face of a stone should be examined carefully before placing the stone in the wall. The stone must have a solid base to rest well on the bed of stones under it. A flat top is necessary to provide a firm bed for those that will rest above it. The top and bottom of the stone are its building surfaces. Since the face is all that shows, it is tempting to choose a stone because it is attractive and compromise on the building surfaces. Not all stones are uniform and it may take some practice to pick out its building surfaces and visualize how it will fit in the wall. All that I can say is that the more stone you lay, the more practiced you will become.

Not all stones will lay properly, but that doesn't mean a stone is always unsuitable. There are two ways a stone may be used if it generally meets the requirements but isn't level. One way is to shim the stone so it is level and stable. The other way is to shape the stone. Shimming is the quickest and only requires a small stone that will level the larger one. Be sure the shim rock is hard enough to bear the weight of the wall that is above it.

You may want to shape some stones to fit better or fill a particular design function. Shaping stone is not as difficult as it would appear. Some basic tools will be needed to do the job satisfactorily. Eight-pound, four-pound and one-and-a-half-pound stone hammers are needed, along with a point chisel, cold chisel and a mash hammer. A brick hammer may also prove useful. The stone hammers are used for chipping pieces from a stone. They are all shaped about the same with flat faces, squared edges and tapered heads that form wedges. They have handles ranging in length from that of a sledge hammer down to about fourteen inches.

116

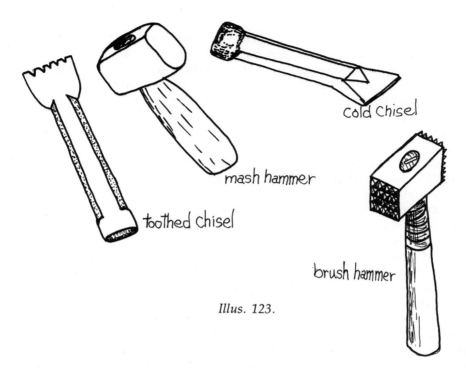

cold chisel

mash hammer

toothed chisel

brush hammer

Illus. 123.

Most chipping is done with the squared edge. Chip small pieces and work toward the size needed. Trying to "break" a stone will probably shatter it. The chisels are for concentrating the impact at a given point. They are good for lowering a surface whereas the hammers chip at corners to reduce the size of the stone or change its outline. The mash hammer is used for striking the chisels. Do not use the stone-shaping hammers to hit the chisels. Keep all of the tools sharp.

Cornerstones and capstones give the wall eye-appeal and balance. Good cornerstones are more difficult to find since they need to have two good faces and a ninety-degree angle. If the corners of the building look good, the whole building tends to look good. Here again, time and patience are a prerequisite if the structure is going to be sound and attractive. I have tried in each chapter to reinforce the fact that all self-builders save money in the same way, through the investment of their time and labor. This is the trade-off for the self-builder without lots of cash.

Capstones are easier than cornerstones to find since their main ingredient is a flat bottom and top. The purpose of capstones is to level the top of the wall to place sills, rafters and other roof components. A common problem with laying stone is the one of planning ahead to the top of the wall. If you look around, you will find a number of walls that look as if they were well planned up to the last three or four courses of stone. From that point on they look as if the mason suddenly remembered that the top of the wall was coming up and tried to find a bunch of small stones to level and complete it. The mark of a good mason is how the wall is capped. The same sizes, shapes and style should be maintained from bottom to top of the wall.

As mentioned earlier, one of the main problems of early masons was that of fitting the stones closely enough to keep out wind and insects. Mud was first used to fill the gaps in the stones. This mixture of clay and water was convenient since

117

the material was found on site and the price was right. The main problem with this material was that it eroded from rain, condensation, frost and time. The mixture was truly mud and the name carried over into today's use of mortar. A mortar of lime and sand was eventually discovered. This mortar had the ability to leach into cracks and was plastic enough to survive some settling. Many stone structures are standing today that are over one hundred years old and still have their original lime mortar intact. Lime mortar is not very water resistant and eventually washes away or becomes crumbly and falls out.

Portland cement was developed about one hundred years ago and due to its composition, becomes nearly as hard as the stone being laid. This is also a reason some masonry becomes weakened. As mentioned, some masons use cement for filler instead of looking for a stone of proper size to fill the space. Also, some masons use cement as a glue to hold poorly shaped stones in place when they should not have been used at all. The good points about cement are that it sets up hard and will not erode. It will bear tremendous weight and is a permanent seal against wind and insects. Cement is not a glue; it will break easily if there is any movement in the wall since cement is very brittle as well as hard.

Portland cement is a powdery mixture of gypsum, lime and clay that has been fired so that when water is added a chemical reaction takes place to combine all ingredients into a single substance. The cement coats the gravel to become a binder while the aggregate gives strength. Concrete must be cured slowly so that it does not dry before the chemical reaction is complete. In warm or hot weather this means keeping the cement damp for several days. In freezing temperatures, the reaction is halted completely, so never use cement in freezing conditions. Too much water in the mix will also weaken the cement. A stiff mix is far stronger.

A mix of one-part portland to three-parts sand is the ratio for a proper mix. Some masons add lime or a fireclay to make the mud more sticky. You may determine the other ingredients that seem to meet your particular needs. Mortar may be mixed in a wheelbarrow, mud box or a mixer. If hand-mixed, use a mason's hoe to save on back problems later. The holes in it let you mix without pulling the entire mess along with the hoe. If you are really into saving your back for other uses, a cement mixer may just be your ticket. Since I am for the use of "appropriate" technology, in my opinion, a cement mixer is appropriate.

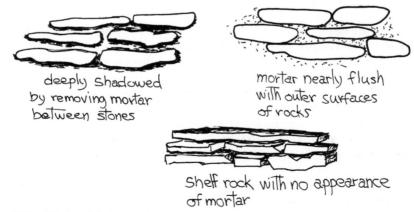

deeply shadowed by removing mortar between stones

mortar nearly flush with outer surfaces of rocks

Shelf rock with no appearance of mortar

Illus. 124. Mortar joints.

Add the ingredients and mix them thoroughly. Add water as needed. Remember, watery cement is weak and it will not provide a good bed for the stones to sit on. A good batch of mud should be stiff, yet plastic. Add water carefully. One minute the mix may seem too dry and you slop a little water in only to find you have a runny soup. Water should be added in very small amounts. Once you have worked with a good batch, you will never want to be careless again. I like to store my mud in a wheelbarrow since it can be moved as I work and the mud can be stirred easily.

A mason's trowel, margin trowel and pointing trowel will be necessary. Use only the amount of mud necessary to seat the stone on its bed. Too much mud will only squish out and run over the face of the work. Once a stone is laid, don't move it. Movement will break the bond and it will not reseat as well the second time, making a weak joint. Prepare each stone well so that it sets in place solidly without mud. There are several types of mortar joints. Basically, all of the joints involve removing various amounts of mortar from between the stones at the face in order to provide a shadow effect between the stones to accentuate each stone. Deeply accentuated stone gives the wall the dry stacked look for a more natural appearance. Some feel that these deeply defined joints harbor insects and collect freezable moisture. I personally like this type of joint and have found no evidence or erosion due to freezing moisture.

Exposed mortar joints may be finished by waiting until the mortar has dried to a granular texture, then scratch and brush it until recessed to the desired depth. Your pointing trowel and a stiff brush will do this operation best. Scrape off the weeping mortar as soon as the stone is placed and do the pointing, as discussed. One of the marks of a good mason is how he finishes the joints in his stone work. Again, take your time and clean the stone faces thoroughly while silhouetting the stones as you desire. When the wall is completed, clean any remaining stains created from mortar using a solution of hydrochloric acid (one part acid to seven parts water). Apply the solution with a long-handled scrub brush. The acid dissolves the lime in the mortar and disintegrates the cement. It is extremely caustic so use it with care. After the cement stains are removed, wash the wall with clean water. If stains remain, use less water with the acid.

WINDOWS AND DOORS

The sides of windows and doors present no special problem other than making it necessary to carefully select stones that make a flush opening. The tops are another matter. Once again you cannot defy gravity so some means of supporting the stone over a window or door is necessary. There are two methods of bridging the opening. One involves the lintel, solid support piece upon which stone may be placed. The lintel may be a long stone or a piece of steel heavy enough to support the weight that will be imposed on it.

The second method is to form an arch over the window or door by using the stone that you are laying in the wall. These stones have to have the correct size and shape to maintain even compression of the arch. The arch stones will have to be supported by a form until the keystone is laid. The keystone is wedge shaped to fit the top opening without falling through. The other stones lean against this keystone being pulled tightly together by gravity.

119

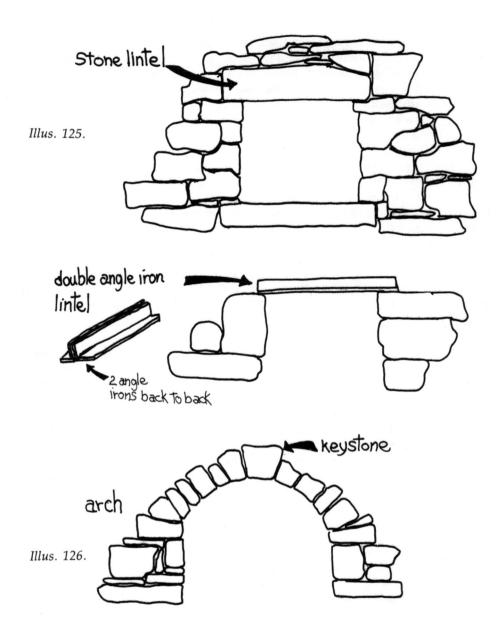

Stone lintel

Illus. 125.

double angle iron
lintel

2 angle
irons back to back

keystone

arch

Illus. 126.

INSULATION

Do not think that a thick wall of stone will safeguard you against heat or cold. Stone is highly conductive and since heat moves to cold through conduction, your heated air inside will be transmitted to the outside in winter and the hot air outside will conduct inside during the summer. Due to its mass, the process will be slow, but it will happen without an insulation barrier. There are several means of insulating a stone wall. Illus. 127 and 128 depict these methods more readily than words, so I will only state that the choice is yours as to how best to insulate in your given circumstances, but insulate!

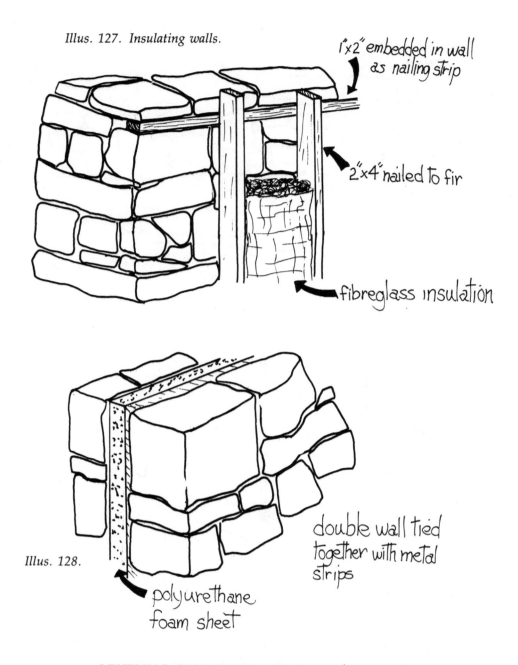

Illus. 127. Insulating walls.

1"x2" embedded in wall as nailing strip

2"x4" nailed to fir

fibreglass insulation

Illus. 128.

double wall tied together with metal strips

polyurethane foam sheet

LEVELING, PLUMBING AND SIGHTING AIDS

The drawings of simple devices and techniques will be invaluable to you once you begin preparing to lay a wall. I find that a level and straightedge are valuable tools. String and corner blocks will keep the wall straight. A plumb line attached to a movable frame will aid in keeping the wall vertical. A hose water level will assure that the entire length of the wall is level. A center post with a measured string is the only device needed to keep a circular wall in perfect curve. Leveling a curved wall can be done by using a long level and straightedge.

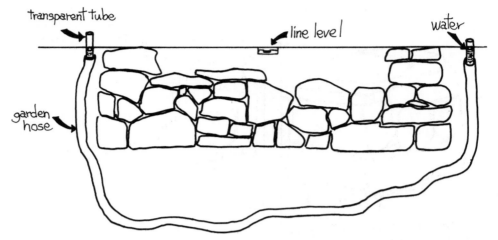

Illus. 129. Hose water level.

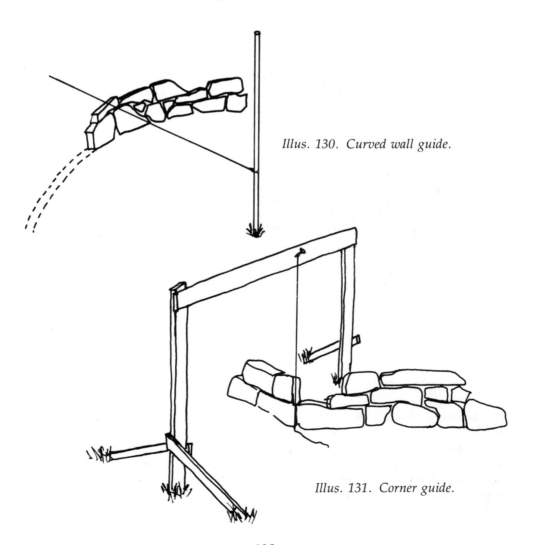

Illus. 130. Curved wall guide.

Illus. 131. Corner guide.

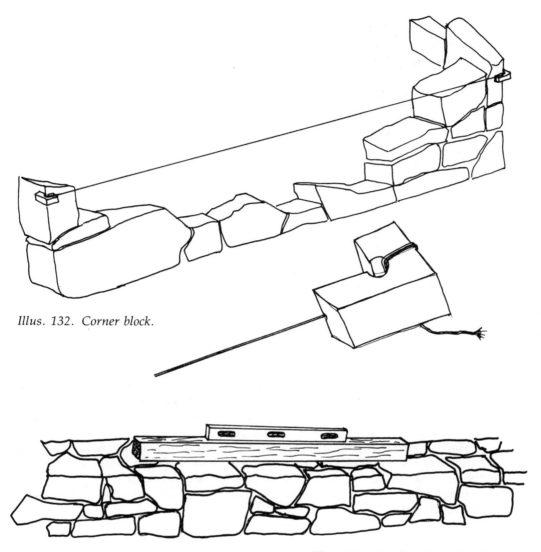

Illus. 132. Corner block.

Illus. 133. Level and straightedge.

STONE FACINGS

A majority of the self-builders plan to move onto their land in early spring, camp out and build their structure in one summer. A stone home that is laid will probably not be completed in this amount of time. Due to the labor-intensive nature of stonelaying, a portion of those desiring to have a stone home reach a compromise. This compromise sometimes results in building a frame structure then facing it with stone. This process requires less time, labor and material. The advantages of a faced structure are that only one side of the wall needs work and you have a solid wall to work against so that the wall is self-aligning. Since a faced

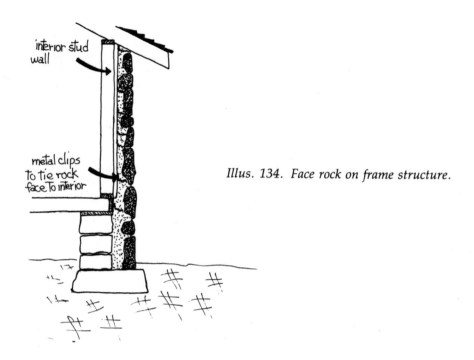

interior stud wall

metal clips to tie rock face to interior

Illus. 134. Face rock on frame structure.

wall is usually for aesthetics, greater attention can be paid to appearance instead of structural detail. Although the stone is not structural, it still is a maintenance-free, permanent wall covering that will protect the structure better than any other I can think of.

The fact that the faced wall is not a load-bearing wall still does not mean that it is not heavy on its own. The result of using a stone facing is the need for an extra-wide footing or separate footing just for the facing. It is best to have a common footing for the structural wall and the facing. This helps tie the two walls into a single unit.

Illus. 135. Block backing.

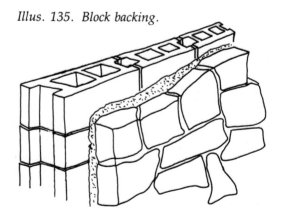

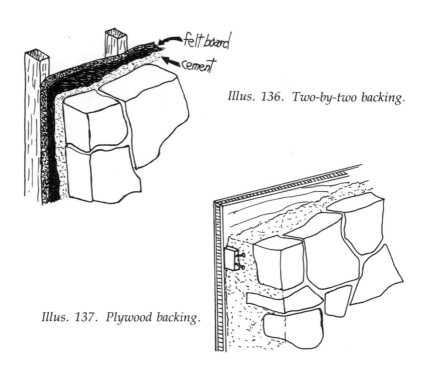

Illus. 136. Two-by-two backing.

Illus. 137. Plywood backing.

Almost any type of a wall may be faced with stone. All that is needed is a straight, plumb wall to build against. Metal fastening strips hold the two walls together. It is good to place insulation between the facing and the wall, along with a vapor barrier. If the existing wall has its own insulation, this will not be necessary. Facing may be a thin veneer only an inch thick or a free-standing wall a foot thick. This wall can actually become a structural wall by using one-by-ones nailed lightly to plywood sheets that become a backing while laying the stone facing. When the wall is finished, the plywood is removed leaving the one-by-ones embedded in the stone wall for use as firring strips to nail drywall or other finish material to.

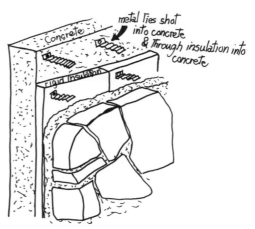

Illus. 138. Fastening face rock ties to masonry or concrete backing.

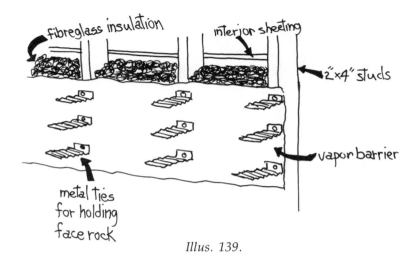

Illus. 139.

The general principles of a laid wall should be applied to a faced wall even though it is not necessarily a support wall. The face rock still has to support its own weight from the bottom up and the mortar that embeds them. Be sure all of the facing stones have flat tops and bases so that they support each other. Backfill the facing pieces with mortar and rubble. Illus. 138 and 139 point out the details of using the wall ties and the various methods of facing. Facing is probably the least complicated form of masonry for the beginner.

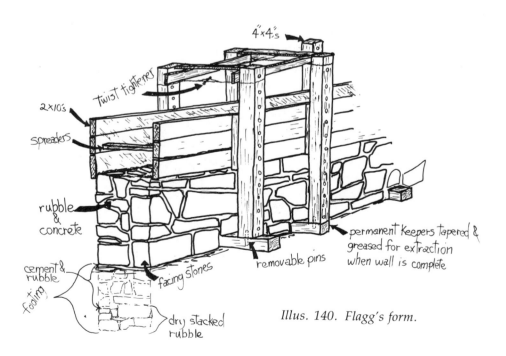

Illus. 140. Flagg's form.

double forms extend around entire structure

bottom forms can be set on those above

constructed from 2"x4's & ½" plywood sheets (each section is 2'x8')

Illus. 141. Nearing's forms.

FORMING AND POURING

Desiring a less tedious and time-consuming method of stone masonry, a man by the name of Goodrich developed the first movable form to create stone and cement-formed walls. As with all forms of construction each person who builds improves on the methods of those before. Formed masonry is no exception to this principle. The early forms developed by Goodrich, Fowler and later by New York architect Ernest Flagg at the turn of the century were very heavy timber affairs that were difficult to build and required a large amount of lumber. These men all felt that the form work had to be left on the wall until the work had set. This meant that the form work had to extend around the entire structure so that a course of stone and cement could be laid or formed.

Flagg improved on the system by using pins instead of nails to secure the planks to the uprights. This allowed the planks to be moved up the wall, thus reducing the lumber requirements. Flagg also made use of the uprights to support ramps and scaffolding. He brought the state of the art to its most usable form as he pursued his dream of economic stone housing for the general population.

Peters, another architect, recognized the major flaw in the existing systems and sought to eliminate it. Having to erect a frame wall against the inside of the stone work, furring seemed a needless expense. The earlier methods called for embedding wood strips into the wall as it was formed to have something to nail to later. Peters used insulating sheathing on the inside of the form held in place by bolts cast into the wall with the stone. He used Celotex. Urethane insulating sheets which are now available would have improved his technique but it was a large advance over the other systems. Peters also worked from piles of materials in the center of the structure which greatly speeded work.

Helen and Scott Nearing made further advances and their book, *Living the Good Life,** has had a tremendous influence on the self-building of stone-formed homes. Scott Nearing has been a social reformer throughout his long life and has always sought ways to help people become less dependent on a highly organized environment of ever-increasing cities. The Nearings have lived the self-sufficient life to an extent that should encourage us all.

*Scott Nearing, *Living the Good Life*, Harborside, ME: Social Science Institute.

127

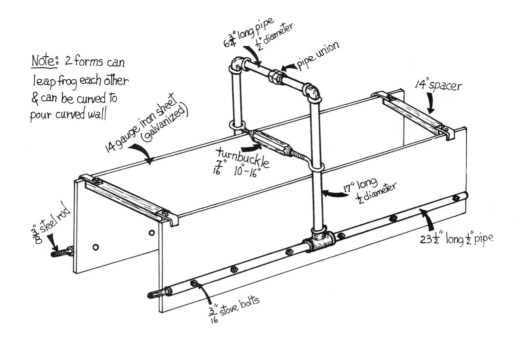

Note: 2 forms can leap frog each other & can be curved to pour curved wall

6¾" long pipe ½" diameter

pipe union

14" spacer

14 gauge iron sheet (galvanized)

turnbuckle
7" 10"–16"
16

17" long ½ diameter

³⁄₁₆" steel rod

23½" long ½" pipe

³⁄₁₆" stove bolts

Illus. 142. Modified Magdiel form (4' overall length and 12" high).

The main improvement the Nearings made over Ernest Flagg's method of stone-forming was the double-movable form. This form consisted of two sets of movable panels that extended around the entire structure. When the first set is poured, the second set is tacked onto the lower set and can be poured immediately. This greatly increases the speed of construction, but the drawback of having to construct the double set of forms with the attending cost makes it less than ideal. If the forms could be rented out for further construction in order to recapture their cost, the system is excellent.

The number of improvements and variations in forms and forming methods are about as numerous as builders. In my opinion, the two most important breakthroughs in formed masonry are the lightweight, portable form and the breaking of the two-day tradition. This tradition dictated that the forms be left in place on the work for two days before moving them. This resulted in having to build a movable form that extended around the entire structure just so it would not take a lifetime to pour the building. To break this time barrier, a light, portable form was developed that could be packed and moved in as little as one hour. By building two of these small, economic forms, the first can be leapfrogged and packed while it is setting up. This process makes it possible to continually move around the structure with at least one course per day. The cement mix is very stiff and sets up quickly.

You will discover additional time- and labor-saving ideas as you start the building process. Be sure to write them down and pass them on to others who are going to build. The following suggestions are from people just like you who plunged in and decided to get their hands dirty.

1. Pile all of the building material in the center of the structure. This makes for shorter trips to the walls.

2. Start all openings in the walls (windows and doors) at the same level and extend to the top of the wall. This will eliminate the need for lintels or arches. It also simplifies forming and speeds up the packing and pouring.

3. Use a set accelerator to reduce water in the mix and reduce drying time. Forms may be moved sooner.

4. Insulate the middle of the wall to give some heat-absorbing mass to the interior.

5. Plan protrusions using natural stone that will serve as shelves and attachment points for other structures. This will be possible only if the wall is to be used without other surfacing.

6. *Don't give up*!

Illus. 143. Laid stone cabin at Cheyenne, Nebraska, built around 1880. Built without mortar and plastered inside, it is a good example of properly laid stone held together by gravity.

Illus. 144. J. W. Peters's Blacksmith Shop built around 1900 in Steele City, Nebraska, is a post-and-beam structure that was faced with native stone.

Illus. 145. Native sandstone cabin. Laid-stone technique.

Illus. 146. Close-up of cabin showing rough mortar joints.

10

Troglodyte Territory

New mortgages and new earth-sheltered homes may be out of reach financially, but you can still experience the earth's sheltering benefits. Perhaps you remember digging hideouts in the backyard or pasture as a child. If so, then you also remember that experience gave a feeling of security and privacy unequalled by any other form of shelter. Perhaps it is sort of a return-to-the-womb syndrome, but whatever psychological handle it is given, the feelings are very real. Although it is possible to tunnel a complete home, the time and labor are substantial, so perhaps a permanent camping shelter would be a good first step.

This chapter deals with the mechanics of safely tunneling shelter in raw earth as well as the basic rules for building an earth-sheltered dwelling. There are two types of earth-protected dwellings. The most direct is that of tunnelling or removing soil in such a manner that the interior space is self-supporting. This technology has been passed down from very early history. The earliest tunnels were created when the surface supply of flint for creating tools ran out and it had to be mined. As the population and need for this hard stone grew, so did the tunnel systems that mined it.

Illus. 147. A cut-and-cover earth shelter (excavation, building, earth backfilled over structure).

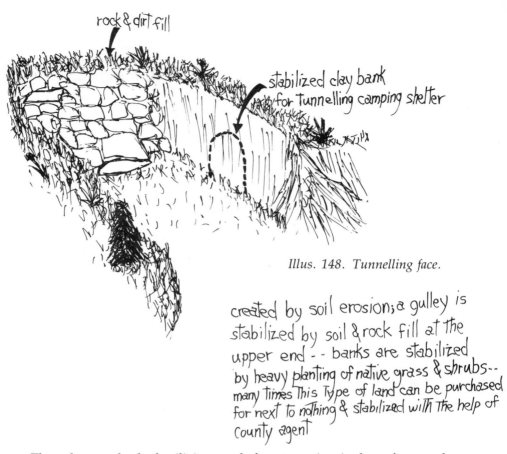

rock & dirt fill

stabilized clay bank for tunnelling camping shelter

Illus. 148. Tunnelling face.

created by soil erosion; a gulley is stabilized by soil & rock fill at the upper end -- banks are stabilized by heavy planting of native grass & shrubs-- many times this type of land can be purchased for next to nothing & stabilized with the help of county agent

The other method of utilizing earth for protection is that of cut-and-cover construction. This method removed earth from an excavation where a building is assembled, then the earth is back-filled around and over several or all sides of the structure, which becomes the support for the soil load. The structure then has to be able to withstand the loads imposed on it by the heavy earth load.

The costs of vacations rise each year, so the advantage of a permanent camp away from the commotion of population becomes more evident. There are many isolated and nonproductive pieces of land going up for tax sale each year. I have seen wooded acreages just outside of convenient commuting range of populated areas sell for as little as $50 per acre. Five acres of wooded, eroded land makes an ideal hideaway, especially if the shelter can be concealed and blend with the land. This keeps curiosity seekers from invading your privacy. A tunnelled sanctuary accomplishes this nicely while also keeping you cool in summer and warm in winter and at a price that is within range of everyone—free.

This form of shelter seems primitive, but it can be made about as elaborate as desired. Many people hesitate to dig a shelter due to claustrophobia and a fear of cave-ins. Although these fears are very real, the reasons for them are not. Thousands of coyotes, foxes, wolves and other animals tunnel their shelter and are never killed in a cave-in. Millions of people live in tunnelled housing in China, Russia, Spain and other countries. Choosing the right soil to tunnel in and the proper shape of excavation to dig are the keys to safe tunnelling. Claustrophobia is no worse in a tunnelled shelter than in an enclosed office or working space. It is

Illus. 149. Tunnelled shelter in excavated face.

all a matter of mental acceptance of whatever surrounding we find ourselves in at the time. The added feelings of security and tranquility derived from a tunnelled shelter will go a long way towards overcoming any negative feelings.

These benefits plus many other pleasurable experiences can be yours for just the cost of your time and energy. Creating a tunnelled camping shelter with a thriving natural environment that can be handed down for generations as a living trust is also a good way to involve the entire family in a constructive activity that beats the boredom of summer reruns on TV.

The main qualities to look for when selecting soil suitable for tunnelling are: density or compaction, uniformity and stability. Most clays make good tunnelling soil. Clay is a finely textured soil that is plastic when wet and hard as stone when dry. An ideal soil mix would be seventy percent sand and thirty percent clay in a highly compacted form. Avoid loess, a yellowish-brown loam deposited by the wind. Although this soil may appear to be substantial, when it gets wet, it dissolves before your very eyes.

The ideal physical site would include the soil mentioned and a face with enough height to allow six feet of overburden above the top of the proposed arch of the tunnel. Often, erosion has already created such a vertical face. If there is no such face on the land you propose to buy, but it has a substantial rise in elevation, a face may also be excavated. This just takes more digging. When you locate a seemingly good site, use a soil auger to take samples down to the depth of the bottom of the proposed tunnel. This will give you an idea as to the consistency of the soil and digging conditions along the route the tunnel will follow. Hidden rocks, water or loose sand will be discovered by this method. If the conditions are questionable, have the soil analyzed and hire or barter for the services of a mining engineer. This is not as expensive as it might seem. Engineering departments of universities and colleges are good resources for this help. Frequently a class will take it on as a field assignment.

Illus. 150. A fireplace in a tunnelled shelter provides good cooking facilities.

134

A tunnelled shelter approximately eight feet wide and fourteen feet deep will comfortably sleep four adults and will not blow down during that unexpected thunderstorm. A center arch height of eight feet is adequate for even the tallest camper.

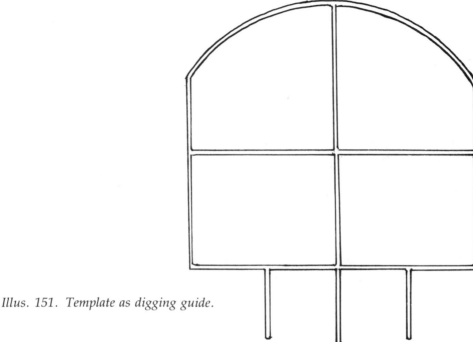

Illus. 151. Template as digging guide.

Start the shelter by fabricating a digging template. This pattern will aid you in keeping a uniform shape to the excavation and avoid overdigging. Half-inch reinforcing rod can be bent to the shape and size desired. If bunks are to be sculpted from the soil, shape them on the template also. Be sure to make the arch uniform since it is this uniform shape that provides for even distribution of the load over the span of the arch and the even compression that strengthens the arch. If the arch is uniform, the more overburden, the stronger it becomes. This compression tightens each molecule against the other.

You will need some basic hand tools to accomplish the digging. A mattock, tile spade, shovel, wheelbarrow and level can usually be purchased very reasonably at farm sales, garage sales and junk stores. Once you are on site with tools and a happy bunch of volunteer diggers, trace the shape of the template on the dirt face and begin digging at the top of the arch. Once an opening has been established, the progress of your digging will become quite tangible.

At this stage of your digging, think carefully about any built-in features you would like to incorporate within the structure. The sculpted bunks carved from the clay in the Mother Earth camping shelter save the cost and bother of cots or wood bunks. Other amenities such as candle sconces, fireplaces, storage nooks, closets and wood storage may also be sculpted from the clay. Remember though that once the soil has been removed, it cannot be replaced in its original form of compaction.

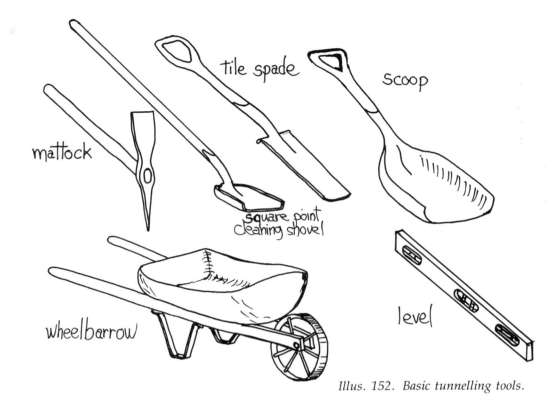

Illus. 152. Basic tunnelling tools.

Carefully draw out the things to be sculpted on paper and plan ahead for the soil removal. Digging is hard work so don't get overtired and hurry, because the result will be less than you hoped for. Take your time and let the soil talk to you. Don't let the mechanized world intrude on this quiet labor. The use of a backhoe or front-end loader will look very appealing after you become bone tired. These machines, however, cannot maintain the even shape required to make tunnelling safe. Work slowly and the soil will tell you ahead of time when it is loose, rock-filled or has other problems that only a shovel at a time will reveal. Baldasare Foresteire tunnelled seven acres of underground space near Fresno, California, beginning in 1910. This project included underground vineyards, orchards, a restaurant, a two-bedroom living space and an underground parking garage. All of this was done with the basic hand tools described earlier. Such surprises as colorful minerals, fossils and other artifacts may also turn up as small rewards for your labor.

As your digging progresses towards the back of the planned space, slope the floor upward about two inches. This slope will help drain any spilled water. The eye appeal of the fireplace is important, but so is its efficiency. A properly designed fireplace can be used to prepare the finest of multiple-course meals. Leave a ledge on both sides of the fire pit; these can be used to place a steel shelf that a dutch oven will fit on for baking. Steel rods placed on the same shelf allow you to hang pots for making stew, chili, chicken gumbo and other one-pot meals that will feed a starving army of campers. A well-planned small fireplace in the shelter will provide delicious hot meals and the warm glow that only a fire in

Illus. 153. A cheery fire and a comfortable bed provide snug camping on a cold night.

winter gives, as well as a practical heat source that will keep the shelter cozy in any wintry blast. Since the inside of the shelter will never get below 40°F (4.4°C) no matter how cold outside, a very small fire will more than suffice. Additional small side rooms added later will add more sleeping space and privacy as well as a possible hot-tub room.

Shaping the fireplace is the fun part, but a flue has to be provided to evacuate the smoke. This opening has to be augered from the ground level above downward into the back of the fireplace and careful measurements have to be made

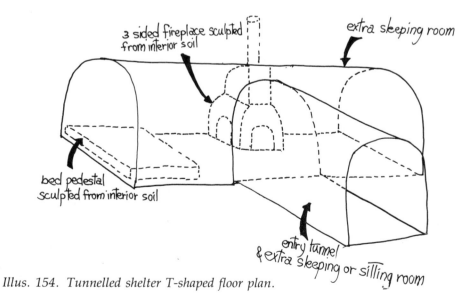

Illus. 154. Tunnelled shelter T-shaped floor plan.

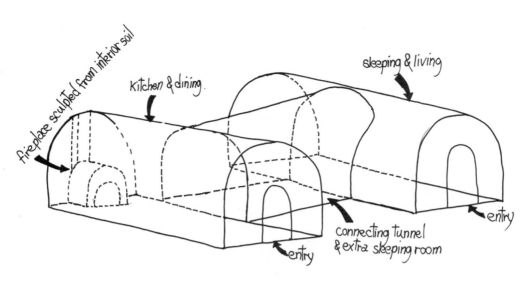

Illus. 155. Tunnelled shelter featuring parallel tunnels with a center connecting tunnel.

from the entrance to the back of the fireplace. These measurements will then have to be repeated on the surface above, being careful to maintain the same line of measurement or direction. A simple engineer's compass will give you the same magnetic direction on the surface as in the shelter. When you are sure of the flue location, drill a small pilot hole to make sure it enters the fireplace at the proper location. A one-inch wood auger jammed into lengths of old water pipe will serve to drill the pilot hole. When you are sure that the flue location is where it belongs, the full-size bore may be started. A four-inch hole should be adequate but if you want a six-inch one, a standard post-hole auger may be used with additional handle lengths to reach the fireplace. A discarded length of grain auger from a

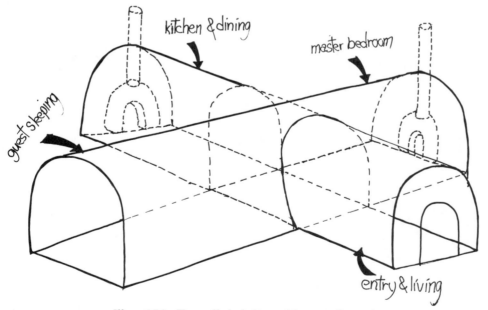

Illus. 156. Tunnelled shelter with cross floor plan.

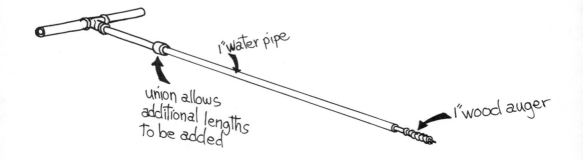

Illus. 157. Pilot auger.

farm may also be used for the four-inch hole. Insert a length of steel pipe that extends above the surface with a rain cap. Cement around the soil when it enters the bored hole. This will prevent erosion.

Your shelter should remain at a fairly stable temperature, ranging from forty to sixty degrees in winter and 60–75°F (15.6–23.9°C) in summer. Troglodytes never freeze or melt! Humidity may be a problem during the summer. This can be resolved by installing soil or "cool" pipes and a thermal vent. Illus. 159 gives an idea as to how these are installed. Any smooth-bore pipe eight to twelve inches in diameter will serve as soil pipe. Each pipe should be buried below frost line and be at least 100 feet in length. This length will allow the hot, moisture-laden outside air to travel far enough before entering the shelter that most of the moisture will condense out on the cool sides of the pipe. The air entering the shelter will be near soil temperature below the frost line. This cool, dehumidified air will be drawn though the shelter by the vacuum created as the warm air near the ceiling is super heated by the thermal vent and exhausted outside through this vent.

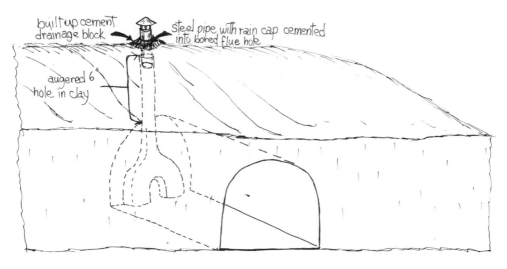

Illus. 158. Flue for tunnelled shelter.

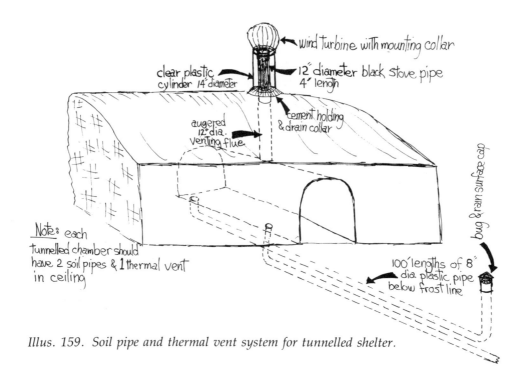

wind turbine with mounting collar

clear plastic cylinder 14" diameter

12" diameter black stove pipe 4' length

cement holding & drain collar

augered 12" dia. venting flue

bug & rain surface cap

Note: each tunnelled chamber should have 2 soil pipes & 1 thermal vent in ceiling

100' lengths of 8" dia plastic pipe below frost line

Illus. 159. Soil pipe and thermal vent system for tunnelled shelter.

The soil pipes draw their air from the outside through inlets on the surface that have insect screens. These pipes enter the shelter at two locations; one at the rear and one near the entry. The thermal vent located near the center of the space and venting through the ceiling will then pull the fresh cool air from both soil pipes into the center of the space and thus cool the space evenly. The thermal vent

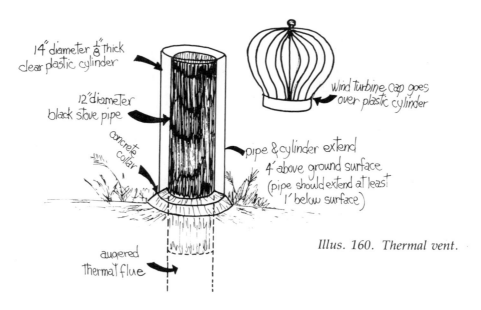

14" diameter ⅛" thick clear plastic cylinder

12" diameter black stove pipe

concrete collar

Wind turbine cap goes over plastic cylinder

pipe & cylinder extend 4' above ground surface (pipe should extend at least 1' below surface)

augered thermal flue

Illus. 160. Thermal vent.

140

hole should be created in the same fashion as the flue for the fireplace. The thermal vent design and fabrication is illustrated in the drawing. There is nothing out of the space age about this cooling and dehumidification system. Systems similar to this have been used for thousands of years in all kinds of buildings. If the airconditioning people find out about this secret we will all be locked away in a giant refrigerator.

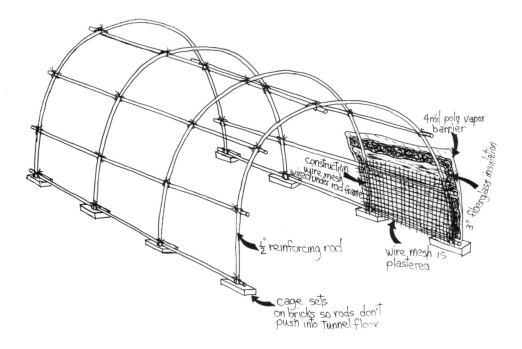

Illus. 161. Plastering frame for tunnelled shelter.

Depending on your own tastes and also on how much use and abuse the shelter will receive, you may want to surface the sculptured interior to help protect it from chips and scratches. If the interior is fairly hard, you may decide to leave it natural. This is a good choice since it saves a lot of work and leaves what may be a colorful and pleasing surface exposed to view. If protection is needed, however, a plaster can be easily applied.

A fine wire mesh can be fastened to the interior surfaces by the use of wire staples. These staples can be crafted out of any wire that is stiff enough to be pushed into the soil. It may be necessary to support the mesh through the use of metal arches spaced three or four feet apart (see illustration). The arches can be crafted from half-inch reinforcing bar that is often scrapped after a construction job. By setting them on bricks at either side of the tunnelled space and wiring them to the mesh, a tunnel within a tunnel is created. The mesh may then be plastered with a mix of the excavated soil, sand and cement. The soil helps maintain the natural appearance of the inside space.

141

I have observed another method of treating the interior surfaces that leaves an absolutely fascinating appearance. Those of you who are potters will appreciate this method since the interior becomes pottery when the process is completed. This vitreous effect is achieved by allowing the shelter to be used as a large kiln for at least three firings. This can be a way to meet all of the potters in the area and make some new friends. The interior is ricked with wood and the pottery arranged on racks. The wood is then ignited and allowed to burn out. If you paint the walls with various colors of glaze, the vitrified interior shell will take on the appearance of a giant marble. Tunnelling can be an artistic means of shelter also. Four firings will leave a shell several inches thick that is as hard as pottery. What a beautiful and permanent method of protecting the interior surfaces.

The last and perhaps the most visually prominent part of your shelter project is the entrance closure. The entrance is the only architectural relief visible on the exterior since this is construction in reverse. Your shelter is created by removing material instead of adding it. If you want the shelter to be as invisible as possible, then an entrance that is fairly concealed is important. If you want to make a statement, then perhaps a stone façade with double-arched doors would be more to your liking. The simplest means of closure is to install a recessed heavy plank door, seed the face with a dense ground cover and add some plantings of shrubs or trees to conceal the opening.

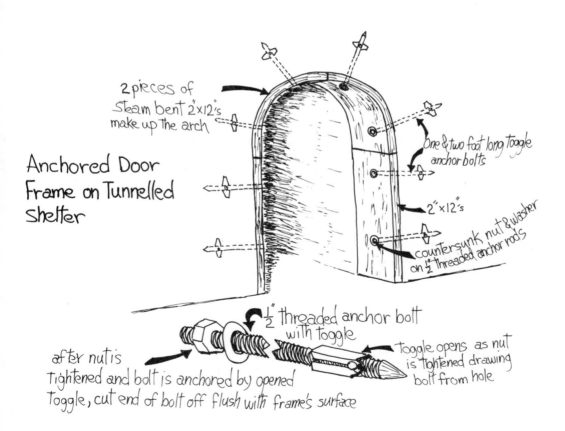

Illus. 162. Anchored door frame on tunnelled shelter.

142

The main problem with the more simple concealment approach is how to best fasten the door frame. The most direct and least technical way is to build the door frame to fit inside and conform to the tunnel opening. The frame may then be anchored to the walls by driving threaded long bolts into the soil. These bolts should be at least a foot long and have a toggle on the end that will prevent them from pulling out. These bolts can easily be crafted from half-inch threaded rod that is slotted near the end for a toggle. Washers and nuts will then secure the frame to the tunnel surfaces. Double-plank doors make an attractive, secure entrance.

Those desiring a more elaborate entrance may prefer something similar to the Mother Earth shelter's entrance. This entrance cost very little in proportion to its beauty and functional use. The tunnel opening was extended forward by pouring an arch of cement that connected with a cement-block retainer wall. This wall, in turn, was faced with rock native to the area. The blocks and cement were the only materials purchased. The stone was indigenous and the soil pipes, flue and thermal vent were recycled or scrap. Mother Earth wanted a more prominent façade since thousands of tourists frequent their Eco Village annually. They also plastered the interior to protect its surface from wear and vandalism.

Illus. 163. Stone-faced concrete and cement-block entrance to Mother Earth shelter.

A retainer wall façade and extended entry tunnel require a substantial footing and dead men anchors back into the vertical face to keep the backfill from pushing the wall outward. An entry of this type is very attractive, but the labor needed to construct it may be more wisely invested in the actual digging of the interior space. Since this is a labor of love, that decision is one of personal choice. Either the natural entry or the façade should have doors that are suitable crowns to the projects. Handcraft doors that will be visually interesting and even artistic.

Illus. 164. Block subwall on Mother Earth shelter prior to facing. Note clips on face for tying stone facing. Center above door is poured concrete tunnel arch that connects to dug tunnel.

Carved relief is always interesting, as are raised panels and a variety of contrasting woods. Since the entire project is actually a large sculpture and a work of art, complete the entry in the same spirit.

    As I mentioned at the beginning of the chapter, an entire home may be tunnelled with space added easily in the future. It would be very easy to complete the camping shelter, move in to it and continue to add rooms by working at your leisure. Unlike conventional construction, tunnelling can be carried on through the winter in comfort since it never freezes in the tunnelled space. As each space is completed or enlarged, your furniture can literally follow your shovel.

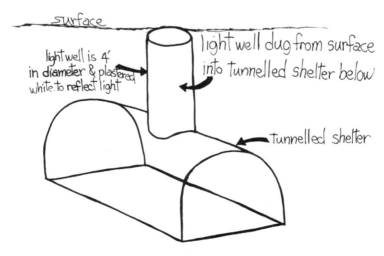

Illus. 165. Light well for tunnelled shelter.

Next to the safety factor, most people are concerned with the lack of available natural light. This is a legitimate concern but need not be since light openings can be placed in a number of locations. The accompanying illustrations show a variety of floor plans and room arrangements that provide for light openings. Tunnelled homes in Australia's opal mining country have every modern feature that homes in the suburbs of America have. Many of these homes even have swimming pools and saunas. The homes were tunnelled in the soft sandstone in order to escape the harsh surface conditions. The following list will provide a checklist when looking for a tunnelling site. It will also serve as a reference as the digging is begun and problems arise.

1. Soil/clay that is highly compacted. Seventy percent sand and thirty percent clay is an ideal soil.

2. Do borings to the proposed tunnel's floor level to check uniformity and locate rocks, roots, loose sand, or water. Do borings along the entire tunnel path.

3. Avoid loess or wind blown, yellowish brown soil since it will dissolve and collapse in heavy rain.

4. The tunnelling site should have enough rise to provide at least six feet of overburden above the highest point of the proposed arch. An existing face created by erosion or previous earth removal will greatly reduce digging.

5. Heavily eroded land grown over with scrub brush and located just outside convenient commuting distance of a populated area will be the least costly to purchase.

6. Check with your County Assessor for land that is being put up for tax sale. County agents, well diggers and rural taverns are also good sources for information on land of this type.

7. In preparing to tunnel, fabricate a template or pattern the size and shape of the space desired and use it to check the uniformity of the excavation as it progresses.

8. A mattock, trenching or tile spade, round-point shovel, cleaning shovel with square point, level and wheelbarrow will be the only tools needed for digging. Construction wire or mesh, half-inch reinforcing bar, plastering trowel, mixing trough and stone-working tools will also be needed if the interior surface is to be plastered and a stone façade erected.

9. Before digging trace pattern outline on vertical face, then begin digging at the top of the arch. Form the arch and side wall a foot at a time. Dig slowly and listen to the soil talk.

10. Plan all features such as bunks, fireplaces, candle or lamp sconces, storage areas and ledges in advance and don't overdig.

11. Bore flue and thermal vent openings from the top down and run a small pilot hole in advance to insure proper location exit in the space below. Dig up a few inches from below after the pilot hole is made. This will prevent a large chunk from being broken out of the ceiling or top of firebox in fireplace.

12. Use engineer compass and level to insure that the tunnel is going in the proper direction and is level.

13. Install soil pipe to enter the interior space at the rear and near the entrance. These pipes should be one hundred feet in length and eight to twelve

inches in diameter. They should be installed so as to drain away from the space into a drain field. The thermal vent should be located in the ceiling near the center of the space.

14. Protect interior surfaces from wear by either firing or plaster.

15. Construct entry closure, either recessed or extruded.

The last part of this chapter will be brief and provide only an outline of necessary information on cut-and-cover construction of an undergound home. The reason I will not go into great detail is the fact that in 1982 I wrote a book titled *Build It Underground* for Sterling Publishing Company and it is in my opinion the most complete reference available to the self-builder on the subject.

As in tunneling, there are steps that cannot be avoided if you are to build a durable, safe, livable and appealing underground home. I will make a list of these steps but first I would like to state my own prejudices on the subject. Having helped design and consult on over two hundred of these structures gives me a vantage point enjoyed by very few in this still fledgling building mode.

As I have repeatedly mentioned, the cost of conventional and high-tech building materials has risen out of proportion to the value of their use and skilled construction labor has followed in the same path. The best way to beat these costs in underground housing is the same as in surface construction; use natural and recycled materials and simple straightforward building techniques that allow the use of unskilled labor.

I will list only one building technique and give the attendant construction steps since it is the most simple and in my opinion, the strongest technique, using the least amount of material while offering the largest number of design possibilities. That technique is post-and-beam with the posts being placed directly in the ground with protective wrapping. This mode of construction gives great strength against lateral and vertical forces and also allows the use of recycled and natural materials as filler. The design possibilities are almost without end and uneven terrain is no problem. Wasteland can be used and a design created to best use its features since no foundation is needed for this type of construction.

CUT AND COVER

1. Make shallow cut (not over one half of the intended wall height).

2. Track the dirt so it can easily be placed around and over the structure.

3. Trench in all utilities placing them in recycled plastic pipe. Frequently damaged irrigation pipe or sewer pipe can be purchased at little to nothing from manufacturer.

4. Use recycled posts at least six by six inches and place them on a base stone for drainage. Wrap the posts in six millimeter plastic wrap being careful not to tear it. This will waterproof and vaporproof the post. If treated posts are used, be sure that the chemical is nontoxic and will not release harmful chemicals into the soil or air. Place some coarse gravel around the bottom of the posts and fill with dirt.

5. Space the posts two to four feet apart around the designed perimeter and at load-bearing points within the structure.

6. Place beams of appropriate size over the posts. These beams will have to support the rafter, roof and earth cover.

7. Run a narrow trench around any sides of the structure that will be exposed. This trench should be below the frost line for your area. Place dense polyurethane insulation sheet two inches thick in the trench. Backfill. This will keep the ground from freezing on the inside of the structure.

8. Plank the outside of structure over the posts making sure that the lumber used will withstand the loads to be imposed laterally by the backfill.

9. Rafter and sheet the roof, again making sure the system and material will support the imposed loads plus an emergency load. Use recycled material as much as possible.

10. Waterproof the exterior by using four to six mil sheets of black plastic wrap. Use at least two layers, being careful not to rip it. Overlap all joints and tape. Be sure to overlap in the direction of natural drainage.

11. Install drain tile and soil pipe using a gravel fill around the entire structure for drainage. This fill, two inches deep, should extend up the walls and over the roof.

12. Backfill by hand being careful not to tear the waterproofing. A foot of soil over the roof is more than enough to sustain plant growth, and protect the structure below.

13. Install all plumbing and wiring between the posts on the inside.

14. Insulate between the posts using six-inch batts of fibreglass insulation.

15. Finish the interior surfaces using any recycled or natural material that is available. Scrap boards of any dimension that are one inch thick make an attractive wall or ceiling when fastened diagonally. Stone facing or rammed earth are other options. Cordwood fill between the posts inside the exterior planking would be attractive and remove the need for the fibreglass insulation.

16. Landscape with purpose, not as an afterthought. Proper placement of deciduous trees and shrubs will protect the façade in summer. Needle trees and plantings will divert wind in winter. Plantings will also insure privacy.

17. Terrascape the backfill to provide berms, bumps, terraces, cutouts for exits and paths as well as recreational areas. The terrascaping is all that will be seen so make it natural and beautiful. I like to fill the entire area with plantings that are not only attractive and functional, but also eliminate the use of a lawnmower. Untold fortunes are spent on water, fertilizer, gasoline, seed and machinery to take care of an artifically created landscape when a natural one that is well planned is just as attractive and labor free. Leave it to nature!

18. Plantings such as trifolate orange, Russian Olive and other dense thorny plants also provide an impenetrable barrier against unwanted intruders.

Follow the basic design principles covered in all of the other chapters concerning function and practicality.

11

In Conclusion

We have covered most of the natural building materials and the various ways in which they may be used to create cheap shelter, along with many design ideas and mechanics. More than anything else, one has to decide what kind of life-style is desired in order to be content with life's routines. The nicest home in the world will be a prison if your are not doing what suits your personality and interests. The things you do to earn a living should reflect your interests. It is so easy to become trapped by the debts we create trying to maintain the life-style that society seemingly expects of us. These debts in turn lock us into living near a job that makes money, but does not satisfy our personality growth needs. It all becomes a vicious cycle until we just surrender.

As I mentioned, you cannot separate building techniques and designs from personality and one's philosophy of life. Life is all interrelated. I do not promote the idea that everyone should run off to the country and live a self-sufficient life-style. The country isn't large enough. What I do promote and encourage is self-determination. If you are a couple and your spouse or companion feels strongly that self-determination is important, the battle is much easier. The main thing is to start cutting the many strings that make us totally dependent on a social system that subjugates us to material possessions solely for the purpose of maintaining a rung on an economic ladder.

Begin to barter your time and talent for return services from friends and small businesses. Trade goods as much as possible. Reduce your debts so you can live on less. You then can pursue your real interests that may not initially earn as much money as a more traditional pursuit. Have patience and set small goals that can easily be accomplished. This will give you encouragement to continue on.

My own life has evolved in ways that I couldn't have imagined as a young person. I started to cut the strings of competitive commercialism after my wife died at thirty years of age. This event in itself made me realize that all of the material success that I had created was pretty hollow. It was at that point I decided

148

that the most important things to me were my personal relationships on a non-superficial basis with other human beings. This philosophical realization started me on a path of learning and interests that I never dreamed possible. In spite of some financial hardship, my life is a continual adventure.

All of this is not intended as a sermon or lecture, but a statement of my own evolution which may parallel yours as a reader. Your interest in alternative shelter and construction techniques indicates your desire for independence.

I have evolved through competitive commercialism in my early twenties to a more people-oriented learning phase. I am now at a point of considering a more mobile life-style to further my learning and be able to better share what I have learned with others.

For almost twenty years I have had a fantasy that may now become possible within the next few years. That fantasy involved the building of a houseboat and drifting down the Missouri River near my home and eventually arriving in the Gulf at the mouth of the Mississippi River. My consuming interest in writing poetry and recording folklore of all kinds may now be the key to this life-style in a modified form.

I have been able to rid myself of all debt and have lowered my needs to a point that my part-time writing, teaching, school-bus driving, designing, consulting and other part-time ventures easily fill my survival and entertainment needs. Hopefully, I will be able to expand my writing of folklore into a syndicated column that I can sell to various small newspapers on a regional basis. This, in turn, would be aided by my being able to travel the 25,000 miles of inland waterways that flow into the Mississippi.

My five-year plan is to be able to launch a replica of a 1910 sternwheel towboat on the Missouri after my youngest daughter graduates from high school. At this point I hope to be able to launch the greatest learning career of my life as well. The unknown people in every village, hamlet and city along these hydro-highways have knowledge about building, gardening, music, poetry, humorous stories, and history tucked under their arms that I want to learn about.

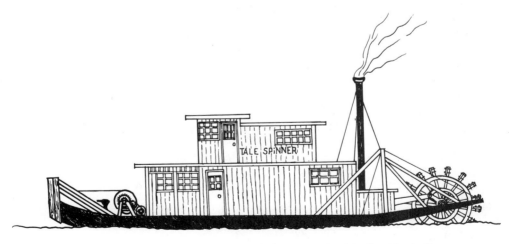

Illus. 166. Replica of 1910 steam towboat, with cypress plank hull with six linear trusses for support (hybrid steam-electric propulsion).

Illus. 167. Home on a barge.

After this long harangue I have finally arrived at the point I wanted to make at the beginning. The one form of building that we have not covered earlier is that of mobile dwellings. Our society is going through another series of changes due to high-tech developments. But the more things change; the more they tend to remain the same. Our society became highly mobile due to the internal combustion engine. Since then because of the sharp increases in the cost of fuel, that mobility has started to decline. Our population became concentrated within large cities due to mass production and marketing from these centers. Now, due to the cost of shipping goods, these production facilities are beginning to decentralize and produce on a smaller scale nearer to the source of consumption. Cities will also decline and smaller enclaves that are more people-oriented will once again grow. The one segment of our population that has seen very little change has been those self-employed persons who chose their life-style. One portion of that group of independents are those who choose to live on wheels or floating homes of one kind or another.

Gypsies were a fascination of many young people when I was growing up in mid-America. Circus people and "carnies" have also held their interest for many. But there is an expanding group of people who, like myself, see an oportunity for enhanced learning and even a source of revenue through their mobility. I have met a number of people like this through Mother Earth's summer seminars. Writers, carpenters, craftsmen and even artists of different mediums live in motor homes, trailers, converted trucks, barges, and other assorted vehicles.

As I just mentioned, the cost of fuel has begun to reduce mass mobility. The ingenious use of alternative fuels and hybrid power plants for vehicles still give the innovative a chance at the gypsy life however. Mother Earth has done a lot of work with wood-gas power, alcohol fuel, gas-electric vehicles and other motive sources. Contact them for additional resources in these areas.

I am considering a hybrid system to turn the paddlewheel on my towboat. A small steam engine using a flash steam system instead of a boiler would drive a DC generator to provide power to an electric drive motor. The generator would in turn store additional electricity for other uses on board through a bank of deep cycle 12-volt batteries. The small steam engine would burn wood trailings from mills along the river. Although this sounds rather complicated, it is fairly compact. The entire drive system would be only a fraction the size of the huge boilers that provided steam for the early paddlewheelers.

Illus. 168. Modern mobile office, featuring extensive passive solar glazing.

I am in hopes of building the entire boat from scrap and recycled material. The parts that I can't get as scrap or recycled will be bartered for as much as possible. My goal is to build the boat for under $10,000. The drawings indicate some of the construction details.

Other possibilities for living on water without motive power are those who build shanty boats and from time to time drift to a new location and live from the river, and garden on shore for food. The July/August 82 issue of *Mother Earth News* has a story about a couple who wanted to live on the Atchafalaya River in Louisiana but kept getting flooded out. Their solution was to purchase a large used steel barge and build a house on it. The entire project cost less than $2,500. They bought the steel barge for scrap at $950 and salvaged a cane worker's home of cypress with two fireplaces for another $450. They now have a large airy home that rises and falls with the river instead of being crushed by it.

The Solar Chariot often seen at Mother Earth seminars is a truck that has been converted into an innovative living space with all utilities and fuel furnished by the sun. This vehicle makes the rounds of all the alternative energy seminars possible demonstrating the sun's endless abilities to meet man's energy needs without robbing the earth of non-renewable resources. In this case, the man's living space also became a source of income.

Some may choose to have a handmade home of a more permanent nature on a piece of land somewhere and be mobile only part of the year. This is another option requiring a less elaborate mobile living space. *Popular Science* ran an article on a handmade, high-tech mobile home that created and stored its heat and coolant while also providing its own electricity. Its shell was fabricated from the split domes of metal grain storage buildings. These were heavily insulated by polyurethane foam. Solar cells created electricity and stored it in batteries. This would be a project for a high-tech personality who is a good scrounger.

In conclusion, don't let convention dictate your tastes and let your imagination and creativity have a run.

Imagination's Door --- Please Enter

METRIC EQUIVALENCY CHART

MM—MILLIMETRES   CM—CENTIMETRES

INCHES TO MILLIMETRES AND CENTIMETRES

INCHES	MM	CM	INCHES	CM	INCHES	CM
⅛	3	0.3	9	22.9	30	76.2
¼	6	0.6	10	25.4	31	78.7
⅜	10	1.0	11	27.9	32	81.3
½	13	1.3	12	30.5	33	83.8
⅝	16	1.6	13	33.0	34	86.4
¾	19	1.9	14	35.6	35	88.9
⅞	22	2.2	15	38.1	36	91.4
1	25	2.5	16	40.6	37	94.0
1¼	32	3.2	17	43.2	38	96.5
1½	38	3.8	18	45.7	39	99.1
1¾	44	4.4	19	48.3	40	101.6
2	51	5.1	20	50.8	41	104.1
2½	64	6.4	21	53.3	42	106.7
3	76	7.6	22	55.9	43	109.2
3½	89	8.9	23	58.4	44	111.8
4	102	10.2	24	61.0	45	114.3
4½	114	11.4	25	63.5	46	116.8
5	127	12.7	26	66.0	47	119.4
6	152	15.2	27	68.6	48	121.9
7	178	17.8	28	71.1	49	124.5
8	203	20.3	29	73.7	50	127.0

YARDS TO METRES

YARDS	METRES	YARDS	METRES	YARDS	METRES	YARDS	METRES	YARDS	METRES
⅛	0.11	2⅛	1.94	4⅛	3.77	6⅛	5.60	8⅛	7.43
¼	0.23	2¼	2.06	4¼	3.89	6¼	5.72	8¼	7.54
⅜	0.34	2⅜	2.17	4⅜	4.00	6⅜	5.83	8⅜	7.66
½	0.46	2½	2.29	4½	4.11	6½	5.94	8½	7.77
⅝	0.57	2⅝	2.40	4⅝	4.23	6⅝	6.06	8⅝	7.89
¾	0.69	2¾	2.51	4¾	4.34	6¾	6.17	8¾	8.00
⅞	0.80	2⅞	2.63	4⅞	4.46	6⅞	6.29	8⅞	8.12
1	0.91	3	2.74	5	4.57	7	6.40	9	8.23
1⅛	1.03	3⅛	2.86	5⅛	4.69	7⅛	6.52	9⅛	8.34
1¼	1.14	3¼	2.97	5¼	4.80	7¼	6.63	9¼	8.46
1⅜	1.26	3⅜	3.09	5⅜	4.91	7⅜	6.74	9⅜	8.57
1½	1.37	3½	3.20	5½	5.03	7½	6.86	9½	8.69
1⅝	1.49	3⅝	3.31	5⅝	5.14	7⅝	6.97	9⅝	8.80
1¾	1.60	3¾	3.43	5¾	5.26	7¾	7.09	9¾	8.92
1⅞	1.71	3⅞	3.54	5⅞	5.37	7⅞	7.20	9⅞	9.03
2	1.83	4	3.66	6	5.49	8	7.32	10	9.14

Index